GETTING
AMERICA
RIGHT

GETTING AMERICA RIGHT

THE TRUE CONSERVATIVE VALUES OUR NATION NEEDS TODAY

★ ★ ★ ★ ★ ★ ★ ★ ★ ★

EDWIN J. FEULNER

and

DOUG WILSON

CROWN
FORUM
NEW YORK

Published in the United States by Crown Forum, an imprint of the
Crown Publishing Group, a division of Random House, Inc., New York.
www.crownpublishing.com

Crown Forum and the Crown Forum colophon are
trademarks of Random House, Inc.

Library of Congress Cataloging-in-Publication Data
Feulner, Edwin J.
Getting America right : the true conservative values our nation needs today /
Edwin J. Feulner and Doug Wilson.—1st ed.
p.   cm.
Includes index.
1. Conservatism—United States.   I. Wilson, Doug, 1948–   II. Title.
JC573.2.U6F48 2006
320.520973—dc22   2005025231

ISBN-13: 978-0-307-33691-0
ISBN-10: 0-307-33691-3

Printed in the United States of America

Design by CEMA

10   9   8   7   6   5   4   3   2

First Edition

To our families—first among society's little platoons, and the fundamental unit upon which all good governments are built. From Ed to my wife, Linda, and to E.J., Wendy, and Betsy, and to Emily, Chris, and Wills. From Doug to Karen, Bryan, and Kayleigh.

CONTENTS

★ ★ ★ ★ ★ ★ ★ ★ ★ ★

FOREWORD

★ ★ ★ ★ ★ ★ ★ ★ ★ ★

by Newt Gingrich

Former Speaker of the House of Representatives

I̲N̲ O̲U̲R̲ E̲V̲E̲R̲-̲C̲H̲A̲N̲G̲I̲N̲G̲, challenging, and dangerous world, the
need for the right ideas to solve the most pressing problems that
face America has taken on a new urgency. I have been known to
offer a few suggestions myself, as in my latest book, *Winning the
Future: A 21st Century Contract with America.* But it will take many
ideas to succeed in meeting our challenges.

In the 1960s, *The Economist* wrote, it seemed as if universities would establish a "monopoly over the life of the mind," providing policies for politicians and ideas for journalists. But the
university became a tower of politically correct babble, and governments led by Ronald Reagan and Margaret Thatcher looked
to The Heritage Foundation in the United States and the Institute of Economic Affairs in Britain rather than Harvard or Ox-
ford for advice. Both leaders praised the indispensable counsel of
these respective institutions. I can personally attest to the effective,
farsighted public policy analysis of The Heritage Foundation.

Foreword

As a young congressman, I attended Heritage events at which I learned from renowned experts how to reduce government spending and strengthen our military. In 1990, when I was House Republican whip, I told a Heritage audience of young conservatives that America faced "a turning point in its history," and I listed five goals for a national agenda, including a growing economy, physical safety for all citizens, and replacement of the bureaucratic state—all areas in which Heritage had proposed sound and innovative policies. One week after the historic 1994 elections, when Republicans captured the U.S. House of Representatives for the first time in forty years, I gave my first major address as the future House Speaker at the President's Club meeting of The Heritage Foundation. It seemed appropriate since Heritage had had so much to do with the provisions of the Contract with America. Because of its great impact in developing the Contract with America, I said, "Heritage is without question the most wide-reaching conservative organization in the country in the war of ideas, and one which has had a tremendous impact not just in Washington, but literally across the planet."

And now, this book, *Getting America Right,* continues the invaluable work The Heritage Foundation has been doing since 1973. The book demands readers' attention for three reasons. First, because its recommendations are based on the research and analysis of a world-class public policy organization that has been on the leading edge of the most important initiatives—arguing for the development of a missile defense system, pointing out the serious flaws in President Clinton's health care reform, providing the economic rationale for welfare reform, documenting the benefits to the United States of the North American Free Trade Agreement, and much more.

Second, because *Getting America Right* is written by two experts in the business of solving seemingly intractable problems—

Ed Feulner, the president of The Heritage Foundation, and Doug Wilson, longtime management consultant and chairman of Townhall.com, the leading conservative news and opinion website in America. Dr. Feulner's key role in the world of public policy is suggested by this comment of a friendly competitor, Ed Crane, president of the libertarian Cato Institute: "Ed Feulner is a great entrepreneur of ideas and deserves accolades."

Third, because *Getting America Right* examines every government action or policy through a unique prism of six questions:

- "Is it the government's business?" Washington, the authors say, should do only those things that cannot be handled better by a state, a community, or an individual.

- "Does this measure promote self-reliance?" Too many government programs punish individual initiative and condemn their clients to "permanent dependency."

- "Is it responsible?" *Getting America Right* suggests several ways to reintroduce responsibility, especially fiscal responsibility, in Washington.

- "Does it make us more prosperous?" The authors argue that because of excessive government regulation, too high taxes, and trade barriers, America is losing the economic freedom that is the wellspring of our national prosperity.

- "Does it make us safer?" *Getting America Right* insists, and I agree, that there must be a seriousness in Washington about the perils we face at home and abroad and a commitment to the kind of strength, courage, and resolution exhibited by Ronald Reagan in leading us to victory in the cold war.

• "Does it unify us?" Government, say the authors, should serve to bind us together, not to exaggerate our differences and divide us. After all, our national motto is *E pluribus unum,* not *E pluribus pluribus.*

"If we the people start demanding answers to these six questions," declare the authors of *Getting America Right,* "government will have no choice but to take the right course—one that is consistent with our cherished national principles." The time for us to act is now. The blueprint for our action—yours and mine—is contained within the pages of this remarkable book, one of the most important to be published in this or any other year.

FOREWORD

★ ★ ★ ★ ★ ★ ★ ★ ★ ★ ★

by Edwin Meese III

Former Attorney General of the United States

AMERICANS ARE A PEOPLE of strong opinions who have always debated vigorously the issues of the day. The Founders forcefully debated the provisions of the Constitution at the Philadelphia convention and later in the press through *The Federalist Papers*. Partisans North and South passionately debated the institution of slavery. In the twentieth century, we intensely debated America's entry into World War I, the New Deal, isolationism versus interventionism prior to Pearl Harbor, civil rights, the Great Society, the policy of containment, and the conduct of the cold war.

Uninhibited debate, you might say, is as American as apple pie. Yet no matter how strongly those on each side felt, they endeavored to respect the other's point of view. They did their best to avoid the odious practice of substituting personal attacks for substantive examination of the issue at hand.

As a result—and this is a critical point—these great debates usually produced a public consensus on even the most controversial issues. This was in keeping with the advice of George Washington, who, in his farewell address, urged his fellow countrymen to avoid the dangers of partisan hatred, fueled by political parties telling lies about each other. Whatever their passing disagreements, Washington said, Americans must remain "firmly bound together by fraternal affection."

Another founder worthy of emulation is George Mason, author of the Virginia Declaration of Rights. That document provided the blueprint for the Constitution's Bill of Rights, perhaps the most significant protection of liberty in the history of the world. Mason was a powerful advocate of his ideas, but he was not contemptuous of those who opposed him. He never insulted those who differed with him. Instead he advanced his arguments with reason and persuasion, often winning over those who had initially taken a contrary view.

But what do we hear today in the public square? Bitter charges and countercharges. Shrill language and rancorous dialogue. We are subjected to a cacophony of partisan invective that drowns out the voices of reason and prevents consensus. Inevitably, this rising chorus of incivility has had a corrosive effect on our politics. We have seen a forty-year decline in voter participation in national elections. In the last two presidential elections, fewer than half of eligible voters bothered to vote. It is imperative that we stop shouting and begin listening to one another, for as Edmund Burke wrote, "Rage and frenzy will pull down more in half an hour than prudence, deliberation, and foresight can build up in a hundred years."

My colleague Ed Feulner, one of the authors of this book, has put it aptly: "Our free, self-governing society requires an open exchange of ideas, which in turn requires a civility rooted in mutual respect for each other's opinions and viewpoints. . . . Restoring civility to public discourse is not an option. It is a necessity."

That was certainly Ronald Reagan's way. He refused to engage in ad hominem argumentation. He was confident that if the people were given all the facts, without distortion, they would make the right decision. And so they did throughout the 1980s. Under his leadership, Americans regained confidence in themselves; they ignited the longest period of peacetime economic growth in our history; and they supported a foreign policy of peace through strength that ended the cold war at the bargaining table and not on the battlefield.

It is in the spirit of reasoned and principled discourse that Ed Feulner and Doug Wilson offer *Getting America Right*. Civil in its tone and respectful in its criticism, the book represents an eye-opening (at times shocking) look at how far our government has moved away from the core values and principles that have guided us throughout most of our history. Fortunately, Feulner and Wilson are here to offer the prescription. Much of what they propose is based upon the research and analysis of The Heritage Foundation, an institution superbly qualified to provide such assistance.

The Heritage Foundation occupies a unique position in Washington, D.C., and indeed in the country. At a time when public faith is fading in institutions of all kinds—government, schools, corporations, labor unions, and the media—Heritage is among a handful of public organizations that enjoys increasing public trust. This can be seen in the two hundred thousand members who financially support the Foundation, giving it the largest, most diversified donor base of any public policy organization in America. Townhall.com is also a powerful force for influencing public opinion. The website averaged nearly two million unique visitors per month in the 2004 election. News, opinion, and action are made available to interested readers.

Heritage became a major player in the world of public policy in 1980 with the publication of its monumental study

Foreword

Mandate for Leadership: Policy Management in a Conservative Administration. Its one thousand pages offered more than two thousand specific recommendations to move the federal government in a conservative direction. President Reagan liked *Mandate for Leadership* so much that, at his direction, copies were given to every member of his new cabinet at their first meeting. Some 60 percent of *Mandate*'s recommendations were implemented or adopted by his administration.

Although not as big as *Mandate, Getting America Right* can, I believe, have as significant an impact on American governance, as it seeks to answer the question addressed by every generation—"How much government do we need?"

The authors begin by pointing out that despite the sharp differences and heated disputes, most Americans share certain fundamental principles—free enterprise, limited government, individual freedom, and a strong national defense. They build their lives around traditional American values—fairness, the primacy of the family, the right to be left alone, the idea that the least among us can rise to the top, the conviction that no one is above the law.

The authors propose sound solutions based upon these principles. For example, the national debt now stands at a staggering $8 trillion. *Getting America Right* lists a number of outmoded, inefficient programs that could be eliminated tomorrow without damage to anyone but the special interests that profit from them.

The welfare system initiated by the Great Society forty years ago rested on a tragically flawed premise—that government can guarantee a good living for everyone. The result has been the virtual elimination of individual initiative among welfare recipients and the creation of a permanent underclass addicted to government largesse. *Getting America Right* suggests a different premise for the welfare system—equality of opportunity. And while those who fail should be helped to get back on their feet, their failure is their responsibility and no one else's.

To help promote sound economic policy, Feulner and Wilson argue that we must reform government regulation, rationalize the tax burden, end trade barriers, and open up world markets with one of their most exciting ideas—a Global Free Trade Alliance.

In the field of national security, the authors insist that the national government's first duty is to keep Americans safe from harm. To meet the clear and present danger of global terrorism, they say, we must take those essential, measured steps at home and abroad that will ensure our security and therefore our liberty.

Getting America Right deals with the fundamental concerns of every society—war and peace, order and liberty, prosperity and poverty. The challenges this book addresses, difficult as they seem to be, are not intractable. Just as the majority of The Heritage Foundation's recommendations went into effect two decades ago, so too can the real-world prescriptions Feulner and Wilson present here change the way our government works. The authors are experienced analysts who know the critical difference between the perfect and the good.

Getting America Right is a quintessentially American book— pragmatic and principled—written for those who are concerned about the future of this great country. Its proposals are offered with the conviction that committed citizens can make the difference in the voting booth, at work, at home, in the community, and, ultimately, in the nation.

GETTING
AMERICA
RIGHT

CHAPTER 1

★ ★ ★ ★ ★ ★ ★ ★ ★ ★

We *Can* Push Back

Freedom is never more than one generation away from extinction.
We didn't pass it to our children in the bloodstream. It must be fought for,
protected, and handed on for them to do the same, or one day we will spend
our sunset years telling our children and our children's children what
it was once like in the United States where men were free.
—RONALD REAGAN

WHERE DID THINGS go wrong?

For proud conservatives this should have been the best of times. After all, conservatives are finally steering the ship of state after decades of liberal dominance.

But look what's happening in this putatively conservative era. Look at the extent to which our government now intrudes into its citizens' lives, reaching for ever more power at the expense of individual liberty. Look at the greed and corruption that have produced outrageous pork-barrel politics and government budgets spiraling out of control. Look at the fiscally reckless accumulation of unimaginable public debt that now threatens the nation and the world. Look at how many Americans now look to government for the "quick fix" or for personal advantage.

And all this is occurring at a time when our nation faces a tsunami of dangers—terrorists eager to massacre innocent civilians; uncompetitive economic practices that drive businesses and jobs overseas; ill-defined immigration policies that jeopardize the uniquely American notion of *E pluribus unum* (out of many, one); runaway government growth that threatens to bankrupt the country.

Gloomy as we may sound in diagnosing America's current ills, we are actually optimistic about the potential for effective cures. Some key changes have already begun, giving us hope for the future. What we urgently need is an action plan for building on these changes to make America as great as she can and should be.

Getting America Right, we believe, is that action plan.

Any plan for fixing the problems that plague our government must involve individual Americans. Too many Americans feel helpless in the face of the government leviathan, watching as budget numbers soar, the number of Washington bureaucracies expands, and government feels more and more removed from our lives. But as this book will reveal in real-world terms, government is not some abstract entity with little connection to our lives; it dramatically affects all of us. Simply put, social power is a zero-sum game: When government takes it, individuals lose it.

The growing complexity of government lets bureaucrats and elected officials hide their acts behind an opaque screen, allowing them to escape accountability. *Getting America Right* shows how we can and must pull away that screen—how each and every one of us can demand responsibility and a return to core principles.

And what are those core values and principles? They are nothing less than what has made America great. And despite our hotly contested elections and increasingly rancorous partisan disputes, Americans still share fundamental principles. We still support free enterprise, limited government, individual freedom, a strong national defense, and the rule of law. Most Americans still believe in the Ten Commandments as guides for our individual lives. We still stand for such traditional American values as fairness, volunteerism, the primacy of family, the freedom to worship as we see fit, self-government, and the defining faith that the least among us can rise to the top—but that no one is above the law.

These ideas define our worldview. They are grounded in our founding document, the Declaration of Independence, which insists on equality under the rule of law, natural rights, liberty, and government only with the consent of the governed. Thomas Jefferson credited the wisdom of the Declaration to a higher power than himself: He called it "an expression of the American mind." In short, the United States exemplified the then radical idea that governments exist to serve their people, not the other way around—that nations become great only when they free their people to become great individuals.

But too often, politics trumps principle in our nation's capital, particularly since powerful interest groups, wealthy lobbyists, and angry extremists have come to dominate the political scene. So why do we have reason for optimism? Because those groups do not represent mainstream America. Much as it may bore the jaded celebrities of New York, Hollywood, or Washington, myriad polls show that mainstream Americans overwhelmingly hold dear the time-tested anchors of God, citizenship, and patriotism. Consider these recent poll results:

- 85 percent of Americans say religion is very or fairly important in their lives.
- 71 percent believe the Constitution promises freedom of religion, not freedom from religion.
- 88 percent agree that "schools should make a special effort to teach new immigrants about American values."

- 80 percent of Hispanic parents say it's more important for children to learn the rights and responsibilities of citizenship than to focus on their own ethnic group's customs and heritage.
- 81 percent of all Americans believe immigrants should learn English.
- 69 percent proudly display the American flag on holidays and any other time they wish.

Now it is time to defend and honor—not just pay lip service to—the principles that have always been the strength of our great nation.

WHAT WE BELIEVE

In Winston Churchill's words, "The farther back you can look, the farther forward you are likely to see." Conservatism is not a religion, not an ideology or a political platform. Conservatism is a set of beliefs that prizes moderation, reflection, tradition, and reason; it cherishes the old and valued even as it produces new solutions. It seeks ongoing improvement of a society, but always in the context of an existing cultural system.

Conservatism is thus a broad social movement of diverse but reinforcing beliefs, gathering travelers on the same journey— pilgrims who may argue over the topography of the promised land, but still move in the same direction. To be a conservative is to apply old ideas to new circumstances. As liberal thinking took center stage politically in the 1960s and 1970s, conservatives relied on the time-tested principles and ideas that could be fashioned into constructive change. And these days, it is the conservatives who seek new approaches while, at the same time, preserving enduring principles. In a speech to the graduating class of 2005 at the U.S. Naval Academy in Annapolis, President George W. Bush told the new midshipmen to be "champions of change" and to "pursue possibilities others tell you do not exist."

We would add only one caveat: Change must be evolutionary, not radical or revolutionary. If customs and traditions need to be altered, the new form can't be imposed from on high. People must be persuaded that change is necessary. Humans are too complex for a healthy society to emerge from the theorizing and the social engineering of elites—academics, editorialists, government officials—proclaiming "enlightened" policy. Government of the people, by the people, and for the people, to use Abraham Lincoln's eloquent phrase, requires the active involvement of an informed citizenry.

Yet for the past seventy-five years, the federal government has sought increasing power over the American people, at the expense of many of our traditional values, and it has often done so in a revolutionary fashion. As conservatives, we continue to believe in the empowerment of individuals, and we remain skeptical of government programs that promise utopia. The American people know their own needs and values and can judge what is in their interest far better than any distant bureaucrat or elite authority. Fundamentally, a civil society derives its strength not from big impersonal government, but from virtuous individuals and "little platoons" joining forces to achieve a dynamic social impact. When government steps in to provide a service that private sources could perform, it crowds out private entities that outperform government if left alone to respond to local needs on their own. Small example: The staff and volunteers at the local soup kitchen go on alert when a regular client fails to show up; they can find out what's wrong and mobilize local help to deal with it. By contrast, the federal food stamp program is simply a remote paper-churning bureaucracy, oblivious to the real people it supposedly serves.

First among society's little platoons, of course, is a stable, loving family. A host of formal and informal institutions follow, ranging from neighborhood schools to churches and synagogues to volunteer fire departments to the Boy Scouts to the Rotary Club. What they have in common is faith in America's shared moral order that respects human dignity, inculcates decency, overcomes fear, and inspires people to help one another in times of trouble. We have learned truths through the ages, among them that all individuals seek freedom, that human life has intrinsic value, and that it is unjust to show arbitrary preference for some people over others.

We also know that freedom is not a license to do anything one pleases. Freedom requires limits and responsibilities—to separate the two trivializes the entire concept of freedom, as sociologist Charles Murray has argued. Freedom endures in a civil society only when individuals accept that with liberty comes responsibility. In return for enjoying liberty and prosperity, we commit ourselves to virtuous behavior, notably in defending the worth of other lives, not just our own. And while we join in helping society's weakest members, we expect them to help themselves to the best of their abilities. People on welfare, for example, must try to use the helping hand being extended to get back on their feet and contribute to society. For one thing, what's good for their self-respect is good for society. A healthy society is built by citizens free to create their own destiny—and to use freedom responsibly. When people and markets are free, they tend to remedy mistakes and choose paths to success.

America's well-being grows from our prime asset: our national character—our passion for individual freedom, buttressed by an abiding respect for justice and individual dignity under the rule of law. Any diminution of that asset is dangerous.

We *Can* Push Back

Accordingly, conservatives deplore the rise of the nanny state over the past seventy-five years—the intervention of government in our lives at the expense of character-building families, churches, and the many other community organizations with which we are all involved.

We will never waver in our firm commitment to the principles that Americans have always believed in. Our country must allow markets to flourish, empower individuals to achieve their potential under the rule of law, and support the values that have made the United States the exceptional idea that it is. These principles have stood the test of time, nourished by much blood and treasure, and even the best-intentioned attempt to change them will prove futile. But we are convinced that they can be applied in new ways to solve problems that our nation has never previously encountered.

America is an extraordinary nation—"a city on a hill" in an allusion to the biblical phrase (Matthew 5:14). As the great British prime minister Margaret Thatcher wrote, "America is more than a nation or a state or a superpower; it is an idea— and one which has transformed and continues to transform us all."

America is the greatest single political invention in human history, and we believe that its future health will come from restoring the intent of the framers' brilliant blend of adequate federal power under real restraint. But that can be done only by mustering public support to beat back federal policies that foment betrayals of principle, profligate federal spending, creeping bureaucracy, and individual dependence on government handouts.

We believe these problems flow from the wrong kind of political compromise, the kind aimed to make cozy deals that benefit the few at the expense of the many. We have nothing against political compromise as such. In fact, compromise is indispensable to building productive coalitions and consensus for the common good. Any republic is a mixed bag of disparate interests that can't function without compromise.

It is imperative, however, to fight the bad kind of compromise, the insidious sort that thrives when lawmakers grow cynical or corrupt. The result is familiar—crooked budgeting, gerrymandering, pork-barreling, truth-spinning. The nation risks getting mired in a new Gilded Age, the high-water mark of Washington corruption that inspired Mark Twain to write, "There is no distinctly native American criminal class except Congress."

But we are not pessimists. Some of our conservative colleagues have concluded that politics have failed, and that our existing institutions are so corrupt and decadent that there is no choice but to scrap the old society and build a whole new set of schools, media, medical services, and the like among the ruins. We believe that such fatalism is profoundly mistaken. True, there are deep social pathologies to be healed in the United States, and the expansion of government power in recent decades has stifled individual choice and thus eroded the competition and innovation that have long been the foundation of American life. But rather than despair, we can and must return to the core values and beliefs that built this great nation in the first place.

We have no illusion that this will be easy to achieve. It means awakening the vast group of citizens who have tuned out of the current poisonous dialogue, and calling them back to act for their country on the beliefs they have held all along. And if we can do it, we will have summoned the soul of America.

As a practical technique for holding our government accountable, *Getting America Right* has a chapter on each of six questions that every citizen and every policymaker should be asking and answering about every government action or policy that comes up for discussion. An unsatisfactory answer to any of the six should trigger deep skepticism about what our political leaders are doing. The six questions:

- *Is it the government's business?* In our highly complex world, Washington cannot stay wholly out of our lives. What we want is the least possible involvement, with federal action kept within the limits of constitutional authority. The federal government should do only those things that cannot be handled better by a state, a community, or an individual. For instance, even we conservatives can make a case that it was necessary for President Dwight D. Eisenhower to launch the federal interstate highway program in the 1950s. The nation's roads were inadequate for interstate commerce, and we could have suffered a military disaster if war with the Soviet Union—then a distinct possibility—had required rapid, massive movement of troops and supplies. The states had neither the expertise nor the resources to create a national highway network. But these days, as Chapter 2 shows, the problem is congestion approaching gridlock—and the federal program is all but dysfunctional.

- *Does this measure promote self-reliance?* Programs should help individuals stand on their own. But far too many government efforts—exemplified by the welfare system and public-housing programs dating back to Lyndon Johnson's War on Poverty—punish individual initiative and condemn their hapless recipients to permanent dependency. The underlying problem is a well-meaning but misguided insistence that outcomes must be equal—that government should ensure that everyone ends up in the same condition. The real objective, as Chapter 3 points out, should be equality of opportunity: Everyone should have the same chance to succeed. Those who fail should be helped back onto their feet, but their failure is their own responsibility if they have had a fair start. Again, quoting Ronald Reagan, "Government can and must provide opportunity, not smother it; foster productivity, not stifle it."

- *Is it responsible?* Programs must be able to stand on their own and withstand the scrutiny of citizens and legislators. Above all, they should not destroy what they pretend to safeguard. It is human nature to be irresponsible sometimes, which is why we have governments to pass and administer laws that protect us from one another. But governments can be feckless too and ours, sadly, is no exception. Our federal government has become so bloated from pork and wasteful spending that it has trouble getting off the couch to act in times of genuine need. Lawmakers are unable to see the difference between high-priority spending—such as rebuilding the bridge over Louisiana's Lake Pontchartrain destroyed by Hurricane Katrina—and vanity projects like the infamous "bridge to nowhere" in Alaska. Our government grows bigger by the minute, we have made vast unfunded promises in public education and Medicare benefits, and the national debt has mushroomed by more than 42 percent. But, as we write in Chapter 4, it is not too late to prevent disaster, and we suggest several measures to reintroduce responsibility in Washington.

- *Does it make us more prosperous?* Prosperity is an intrinsic ingredient of the American Dream, one that our republic achieved to the world's envy. But in recent decades, our government has switched from promoting sound economic policy to dishing out advantages to special interests—and in the process, our economy has become weighted down with handicaps. Outmoded and unneeded federal programs, layers of regulation, and favors for the powerful soak up resources and erode our competitive position just as the globalized business world demands ever-greater efficiency and creativity. In short, we are losing the economic freedom that is the very wellspring of national prosperity. To regain it,

Chapter 5 proposes that we reform government regulation, lighten and rationalize the tax burden, end all trade barriers, and open up world markets with a Global Free Trade Alliance.

- *Does it make us safer?* Governmental policy should protect our country and make for a better future. Keeping America safe from harm is any president's—indeed, any government's—first duty. And there is no shortage of threats to guard against. We face an insidious and implacable band of fanatical terrorists who do not hesitate to sacrifice their own lives—and those of their hapless relatives, friends, and neighbors—to weaken our national resolve. We face rogue states that support terror and try to sneak into the nuclear weapons club to blackmail us and aggrandize their own power and influence. And we see a potential world rival, China, whose exploding economic strength is being used to build up its armed forces with the world's second-largest military budget. These are largely uncharted waters, and we have made more than our share of mistakes and miscalculations in trying to navigate them. But we are still winning on balance, and, as Chapter 6 makes clear, it is not too late to correct our course. What's needed is a new seriousness in Washington about the perils we face and the end of business as usual in providing security, buttressed by the kind of strength, courage, and resolution that Ronald Reagan brought to bear in his final defeat of the Soviet Union.

- *Does it unify us?* Government should bind us together with our shared national values, not exaggerate our differences and undermine our national identity, principles, and purpose. Our country grew by gathering a great human stew of Puritans, gamblers, and second sons; of fugitives, dreamers, and the dispossessed. They miraculously forged themselves into "Americans" with a common identity and set of values. Our unofficial yet vital symbol, the melting pot, turned base metals into one of the strongest alloys on earth. But today that alloy needs reinforcing, mainly because we have lately taken to celebrating "diversity" and encouraging differences. No one advocates prejudice and intolerance, yet no one should tolerate favoritism or inequity. When we permit people to become citizens and still think of them-selves first as Chinese, Mexicans, Iranians, or Nigerians—"hyphenated Americans," as Theodore Roosevelt put it nearly a century ago—we risk losing the glue that holds us to-gether as a nation. When we hold some Americans back, we reduce our potential as a nation. Governmental policies and programs, we assert in Chapter 7, must encourage patrio-tism, American values, a common language, a unified na-tional identity, and a level playing field, without fear or favor.

If we the people start demanding answers to these six ques-tions, government will have no choice but to take the right course—one that is consistent with our cherished national prin-ciples, yet innovative in the way they are practiced. To be sure, we are not so naïve as to assume that each of our six standards can be achieved without reference to the others. Like everything in life, these benchmarks are interdependent. Trade-offs are in-evitable. For example, the nation would clearly be safer if we closed every port in the country, but it would also leave us less prosperous. Conflicting priorities like these will necessitate com-promise, and often excruciating compromise. But that's what policymakers do for a living, and we have no intention of allow-ing them to throw in the towel just because their jobs have be-come more difficult than ever.

That said, we believe our six-question approach outlining the right role for the federal government is one of the most clarifying, and certainly energizing, reform ideas ever proposed. With your support, it could well become the bypass operation that restores Washington's failing political heart to normal functioning. It is our hope that this book will show the way.

CHAPTER 2

★ ★ ★ ★ ★ ★ ★ ★ ★ ★

Is It the Government's Business?

Government is not reason; it is not eloquence; it is force!
It is a dangerous servant and a terrible master.
—GEORGE WASHINGTON

BY 1919, THE PONY EXPRESS was ancient history. Iron horses sped huge trainloads of people and products, day and night, crisscrossing the United States on steel rails laid coast to coast. Even so, transcontinental highways barely existed: In America before Henry Ford, driving a flivver across the West was often slower and less reliable than riding your own quarter horse, much less taking the train.

As World War I ended, a young army officer spent a miserable chunk of 1919 getting a sour taste of America's primitive roads. He was Dwight D. Eisenhower, a twenty-nine-year-old West Pointer trained in the new art of tank warfare. Eisenhower's specialty got him assigned to the army's first cross-country road trip (tanks need commanders who know the fastest way ahead). On this mission, eighty-one military vehicles were assigned to drive from Washington, D.C., to San Francisco as rapidly as possible. But once they got past Ohio, the caravan slowed to a crawl in what seemed a limitless land of deep mud, thick dust, hairpin curves, and windswept prairies. The trip took sixty-two days—an average of fifty-eight miles a day. A train would have been at least twelve times faster and infinitely plusher.

Like the Romans, the future General Eisenhower never forgot the military's need for superb roads. As Allied commander during World War II, some twenty-five years later, he was impressed with how fast his troops could move over Germany's autobahns. As president in the 1950s, he saw a major military need for modern U.S. highways to deploy the country's defenders in the then plausible case of war with the Soviet Union. Accordingly, he persuaded Congress to embark on a massive federal project to build an interstate highway system—a clearly legitimate use of Washington's aid because of its constitutionally mandated national defense obligation and because the project also promoted interstate commerce.

Launched in 1956 for the then staggering sum of $27 billion, 90 percent paid by the federal government, the result was a forty-one-thousand-mile network of interstate highways connecting major population centers—a boon for U.S. commerce and defense. Devoid of traffic lights from coast to coast, the interstates were brilliantly designed. Long stretches were even deliberately curved every mile or so to keep drivers awake and alert.

Today, with the Soviet Union long gone, the country's interstate highway problem is not invasion but congestion. So who's responsible for funding ever more needed highway capacity? Absent a clear and present national danger, are highways really Washington's business?

Most Americans still take it for granted that the federal government is the rightful sugar daddy of highway funding. But that assumption doesn't bear much scrutiny. Few seem to be aware of how Congress actually apportions the 18.4-cent federal tax we pay with every gallon of gas we pump. In fact, the tax is literally earmarked for highway robbery. Nearly a quarter of the money is set aside not for needed highway expansion, but for transit systems that carry only 1.8 percent of travelers, plus thousands of pork projects aimed at massaging local voters in order to get members of Congress reelected.

For example, Don Young, Alaska's Republican chairman of the House Transportation and Infrastructure Committee, bedecked the 2005 highway bill with two bridges, at a total cost of more than $450 million. One would link the town of Ketchikan, in southeastern Alaska, with an island a mile offshore. The island has a few dozen residents and a small airport. The second bridge would run from Anchorage to Port Mackenzie. If that seems extravagant, the bridges will have roads that at least carry cars. Another tidbit in the highway bill provides $3.5 million for horse trails in Virginia.

From 1998 through 2003, the federal government spent $217 billion for "transportation," but to little avail for motorists, the supposed main beneficiaries. Only a fraction of the money produced new road capacity. Given population growth, the misspending instead produced more and more traffic congestion, especially in fast-growing states like Arizona, California, and Florida. According to the Texas Transportation Institute, which tracks congestion in seventy-five cities, rush-hour traffic jams snarled 55 percent of cars on the nation's freeways in 2001, up from 43 percent in 1996. By 2001, more than one-third of all U.S. drivers were hitting significant congestion at any time of day.

The double whammy of federal misspending and the states' runaway traffic problems suggests that the U.S. government has effectively squandered any legitimacy it had as overlord of the nation's local and regional transportation. The billions of federal dollars Congress appropriates for bigger and better highways are shamefully diverted to privileged constituents, creating bigger and worse traffic jams for the ordinary motorists forced to finance the mess.

Worse still, the federal law governing fuel taxes has a built-in bias favoring some states over others. In larger, more populous states like Florida and Texas, motorists use more gas and thus pay more fuel taxes into the Highway Trust Fund than motorists in smaller, slower-growing states like Connecticut and Massachusetts. The first group, called donor states, winds up paying more into the Highway Trust Fund than it gets back. The second group, called recipient states, gets back more than it pays in. This system has nothing to do with need or resources; in fact, Mississippi, the poorest state in the Union, is a donor, and Connecticut, the richest one, is a recipient.

Motorists would surely get a better return on their tax dollars if highways were controlled by state governments rather than by Washington. States, after all, are where the roads are, even if the dollars aren't, and it stands to reason that they know a lot more about their problems than the feds do. But let's not leave it there. One of the best solutions to the highway problem, as to so many others, would be a private one based on free-market forces, with limited government involvement of any kind—state or federal.

Among the realities of government bureaucracy at nearly any level is that inertia rules. To most bureaucrats—as Ronald Reagan pointed out again and again—risk taking endangers the dream of retiring young with a hefty pension. Entrepreneurship is folly. Job security means standing (or sitting) in place without rocking the boat. It is futile to expect much creativity from a bureaucracy as large as the federal government.

Creative solutions to problems like highway congestion are more likely to come from free marketeers than from governments. One such solution that illustrates the impact of new thinking about old problems is currently on display in California.

The problem at issue goes back to the 1950s decision to finance interstate highways with gasoline taxes rather than tolls, which were common in the country but politically unpopular. No one wanted tollbooths on the huge new interstates; gas taxes seemed equitable and unobtrusive. In time, of course, traffic soared in urban areas, requiring both higher taxes and new tolls to pay for more road capacity. But there was never enough money to do the job, thanks mainly to highway robbers in Congress.

Desperate for inexpensive ways to ease traffic jams, which were worsened by cars carrying just one passenger, highway engineers came up with rush-hour lanes reserved for cars with two or more passengers. These were supposed to encourage pooling and thus thin out traffic in regular lanes. And so they did, but poorly. Around cities like San Diego, it became common for solo commuters to sit in stalled traffic and look morosely at empty car-pool lanes devoid of carpoolers. What to do?

As John Tierney reported in *The New York Times Magazine,* starting in 1996 San Diego's traffic managers invited solo drivers to use car-pool lanes for a price that constantly changes according to traffic levels. Electronic signs display the variable fee at lane entrances. A computer counts the entering cars and readjusts the fee—higher if too many cars accept the toll, lower if not enough do. Between 7:00 and 8:00 A.M. on a typical workday morning, the toll can start at $1.25, jump as high as $2.50, and fall back to $1, all depending on drivers assessing traffic volume and deciding whether the price is worth paying. What makes this free-market experiment all the more effective is that drivers opting to pay needn't even slow down to fork over their tolls. Those with FasTrak responders (the West Coast version of the East Coast's E-ZPass) are automatically charged the going price by overhead radio transmitters that read the driver's account number at speeds more than 100 miles an hour (although not many drivers get to test this system at top speed).

San Diego's high-occupancy toll lanes thin out traffic even

more by allowing free entry to buses and commuter vans along-side toll-paying cars. These lanes are now so popular that the city has extended them twelve miles farther out of town. Indeed, variable-toll pricing is an idea whose time has definitely come: It has lately emerged as the leading anticongestion solution for new tollways being planned for more than a dozen cities and metro areas, including Atlanta and, ironically enough, Washington, D.C.

By charging literally what the traffic will bear, variable pricing offers a powerful answer to this chapter's question: Is it the federal government's business? In this case, the answer is yes, but only partially and temporarily. Back in 1998, Congress funded a pilot program to assess "value pricing" for toll roads in twelve states. At about the same time, a means to collect tolls automatically—the electronic responders, or FasTrak system—was developed. What is now called variable pricing was pioneered by CalTrans, the California Department of Transportation, which owns and operates the state's fifteen-thousand-mile highway system. CalTrans's creative, market-based approach in San Diego enables it to collect sufficient toll revenue on highway I-15 to keep the road in good condition, pay for police, and provide free buses for commuters who leave their cars at home.

As conservatives, we regret that the federal government has anything to do with managing roads in San Diego or any-where else. When politics and bureaucracy intrude on legitimate federal purposes—in this case, national security and national development—stagnation and inefficiency become the rule, special interests prosper, and we the people suffer. Our preference is always and everywhere for private enterprise. But if government has to be involved, say in providing seed money or launching regionwide systems, then it should at least do the job with market-based principles in mind, as is the case in San Diego. Getting free-market principles established in all forms of public service is a high priority.

SEPARATE BUT LIMITED

By neither inclination nor tradition do most Americans expect the federal government to stay altogether out of their lives. What should be expected is minimal involvement: Let Washington be the last resort, the one Americans turn to only when they truly can't devise any alternative—which, given our resourcefulness, should be rare.

As Alexis de Tocqueville, the nineteenth-century French political writer, famously observed in *Democracy in America,* "The citizen of the United States is taught from infancy to rely upon his own exertions to resist the evils and difficulties of life; he looks upon the social authority with an eye of mistrust and anxiety, and he claims assistance only when he is unable to do without it."

Quite true—or so it used to be, at least. And just as self-reliance characterized the first settlers in this country, so the U.S. Constitution exemplified that spirit by creating a federal government of separate and limited powers—one strong enough to represent a new nation to the world, but weak enough to allow states and individuals to thrive. In Article 1, Section 8, the Constitution lays out the specific powers vested in Congress. They range from collecting federal taxes and regulating interstate commerce to raising armies for national defense and declaring war. They also include the power to make all laws "necessary and proper" for carrying out any constitutional power—a way to adapt those powers to changing times. As it turns out, the result has been stacking ever more federal laws as high as the Washington Monument.

On the whole, the Constitution is a marvel of principles and restraint, a unique compass designed to keep the nation both pointed in the right direction and stable in the face of unknowable change in the future. But if we revisit the Constitution's original impetus—the need to preserve American independence and self-reliance—we realize that what the document does not say is no less important than what it does say. For example, it does not mention such activities as education, medical care, and retirement security. These issues and others affect self-reliance in profound ways. The framers excluded them from the Constitution almost certainly because, at the time, most Americans thought they were none of the federal government's business and were best carried out by individual citizens. When this important separation of federal and local functions is breached, problems begin and few people gain. The poor state of our school system is a classic example.

In the 1940s, the country woke up to the inevitable effects of strictly local public school control and financing in a widely diverse nation. Huge differences in funding between urban and rural schools had created vast disparities in teachers' salaries and school facilities, leading to so many have-not public schools with teacher shortages and crowded classes that American education seemed on the verge of becoming an oxymoron.

The misplaced assumption was that the solution was help from Washington—a federal school bailout—which resulted in President Eisenhower's seeking federal money for public elementary and secondary education. Congress narrowly voted him down, partly out of concern over federal control of education. Even so, this Republican president managed to launch the Department of Health, Education, and Welfare in 1953, adding more federal fat. Democratic president Jimmy Carter next split off education and gave it its own separate department in 1979—thus giving life to one of the more intractable bureaucracies the federal government has yet invented.

Since 1965, according to the House Committee on Education and the Workforce, the federal government has spent $321 billion on education, including a 90 percent increase since 1997, compared with a 40 percent rise in overall federal spending. Shouldn't the logical result be all sorts of wonderful academic improvements in U.S. schools?

Sorry, it hasn't worked out that way. Since 1995 test scores for American schoolchildren have fallen steadily behind those of students in Britain, Japan, the Netherlands, Singapore, and most other industrial nations. In 2003, for example, the United States ranked fourteenth out of thirty-five nations in eighth-grade math testing. In other words, it looks as though education ranks among the black holes of federal spending.

The existence of the Education Department is proof that hundreds of public schools in the United States confront ghastly problems that millions of Americans yearn to solve. It is also proof that federal bureaucrats have almost zero chance of truly solving those problems.

It is clearly impractical to demand that the federal government immediately withdraw from education, health care, and all the other areas in which its current vast presence is, to our minds, clearly unconstitutional. It is too late, as well as politically impossible, to try to lock that barn door. The intruders are already acting like owners. But we can, and must, try to keep the remaining horses under local control. With patience, persistence, and citizen involvement, it should also be possible to get back some of the stolen ponies.

LET'S NOT MAKE A FEDERAL CASE OUT OF IT

The problem isn't just that the federal government lacks the sensitivity to handle problems best left to the local people who know them best. What's worse, federal lawmakers and bureaucrats have a tendency to abuse their power in handling such projects. At the extreme, as we've already seen, this produces multimillion-dollar bridges to nowhere. More typically, the result is a flood of relatively penny-ante boondoggles that buy off local constituencies and power brokers at a staggering collective cost to the rest of us. Let's look at a few egregious examples of our government in its "don't just stand there, do something" mode.

Consider the federal program entitled Community Oriented Policing Services, which goes by its acronym COPS. This was President Bill Clinton's plan for putting one hundred thousand new police officers on the streets of the United States. In 2000, Clinton proudly claimed that COPS was the reason violent crime had suddenly begun dropping in this country. We at The Heritage Foundation suspected otherwise. In a statistical study of COPS grants to U.S. counties, published in 2001, we found no correlation between the influx of federal tax dollars subsidizing officers' salaries and the violent-crime decline. The Justice Department's COPS office requested a copy of our data, which we immediately provided. A few months later, and after paying some $160,000 in taxpayer funds, Justice produced its own study by two professors and a COPS employee. The study argued that COPS grants did indeed reduce violent crime.

Both studies went to a Senate Judiciary subcommittee, which, as Delaware's Democratic senator Joseph R. Biden Jr. acknowledged, set out to refute the Heritage study by touting the COPS-funded report. The Heritage Foundation responded by asking one of the COPS-funded authors for a copy of his underlying data. That was in December 2001. Heritage asked again in 2002 and 2003, all to no avail. Administrators at COPS even stonewalled a data request filed under the Freedom of Information Act. At one point, COPS personnel claimed they could not act without permission from the study's authors, as if this government-funded analysis involved some sort of privacy issue. The authors, however, told us that Justice had forbidden them to cooperate.

Eventually, COPS did release the data—but only after Heritage complained to senior Justice Department officials and to members of Congress. We're happy to report that COPS did not survive its own data. Congress subsequently scrubbed the program for being what it truly was—wasteful and ineffective.

In another example of misuse of federal powers, Robert Byrd of West Virginia, the ranking Democrat on the Senate Appropriations Committee, saw to it that his state received $4,337,000 for the establishment of a Geographic Information Center for Excellence (as if the country needs public-sector mapmakers), $160,000 for poultry litter composting, and another $621,000 for agriculture waste utilization, among other goodies.

Patty Murray, a Democratic member of the Senate Commerce Appropriations subcommittee, and Norman Dicks, a Democratic member of the House Appropriations Committee, supported $9,450,000 in projects for their state of Washington, including $2 million to acquire 250 acres on Maury Island, $3 million to protect a smelt habitat off the coast of Bainbridge Island, and $750,000 for the Snohomish County sheriff's office to buy palm-imaging technology.

Once again, by turning local issues into federal matters, Congress robs the taxpayers of other states. It's not only unfair to the rest of the country; it's also unnecessary. The federal government should focus on real national issues and stay out of state and local matters. The more we allow state and local governments to become addicted to federal money, the less creative they become and the worse they govern. Nothing is more pernicious to vibrant politics in this country than permitting our 50 states and over 3,000 counties to beg for Washington handouts, in the process losing their initiative and their creative competitiveness.

Some people disagree. They still believe the federal government is necessarily the best instrument for providing vital social services. That view may have had a grain of truth for the first one hundred or so days of Franklin Roosevelt's New Deal, when the nation seemed on the brink of collapse. But the crisis came to an end—and in any case, that was three-quarters of a century ago. More important, lots of evidence now indicates that such intervention wasn't necessary even then—that the New Deal activism actually prolonged and exacerbated the Great Depression.

In the intervening years, the federal government has built itself quite a reputation as being something of a bumbling idiot with helping hand extended. In Maine, for instance, the feds have been warning about a lobster shortage for the past twenty years. And to combat the perceived problem, Congress slapped on a slew of regulations to limit the lobstermen's catch. Trouble is, rather than being in decline, the lobster population has been exploding. A May 2005 article in the *Wall Street Journal* described "the greatest boom the Maine coast has ever seen. Lobster . . . pumps some half to three-quarters of a billion dollars into Maine's economy each year."

It's not as if the federal regulators were blindsided by a suddenly amorous population of lobsters. The Maine lobstermen, who have long prided themselves on conservatively managing the lobster stock, and who base their population assessments on firsthand knowledge of the catch, pleaded with the federal scientists to recheck their mathematical models and to revise their doomsday data. No dice. Ignoring direct evidence, the National Maritime Fisheries Service (NMFS), which Congress created in 1976 when it passed the Fishery Conservation and Management Act, forged ahead with even stricter regulations.

Frustrated by the absurdity and unable to break through the federal firewall, the lobstermen finally got local scientists to listen to their arguments. A respected group of population-modeling biologists declared in the fall of 2004 that the NMFS was flat-out wrong about the lobster population, and they concluded that the agency's models were unreliable and its data inadequate.

The NMFS comes off as the bad guy in all this, but, as the *Journal's* Trevor Corson points out, placing the blame on the NMFS misses the point: "The real culprit here is ill-conceived and overly ambitious federal legislation, applied to a local industry that was doing a decent job of regulating itself." In other words, Congress should have kept its fumbling fingers out of Maine's lobster pots in the first place.

How can anyone who takes pride in intellectual honesty defend a pattern of federal failure? They can't. Yet the Congress and succeeding administrations seem unable to stop throwing more and more federal money at any and all problems—which only leads to more federal failure. Our alternative embraces an entirely different approach, radical only in that it strives to make practical sense and get urgent work done without miring Americans in more debt and dependency.

THIS WAY TO SERFDOM

The fathers of our country were remarkably sophisticated about human nature. Having no illusions about opportunists grabbing power wherever it's not nailed down, they proceeded to nail it down. The Constitution writers limited the federal government by splitting it into three branches, curbing them with ingenious checks and balances, and generally preventing one from dominating the others. As conservatives, we revere these principles and view the Supreme Court as their ultimate guardian. To be sure, the hugely swollen modern presidency has sharply diverged from the framers' intent. Still, the Supreme Court is supposed to go on faithfully umpiring the system in what amounts to a noble mission—combating concentrations of governmental power.

But does it succeed? Not in the now infamous case of *Kelo v. City of New London,* a classic of the latter-day judicial sophistry that too often produces abstract opinions unrelated to real-world conditions.

Winding up its yearly session in June 2005, the Supreme Court stunned people everywhere by obliterating one of the Constitution's key checks on the government's power to seize private property. At issue was the Fifth Amendment clause, "nor shall private property be taken for public use without just compensation." The question before the court was how the law should define "public use."

State and local governments have long invoked their power of "eminent domain" when private property stands in the way of public-use projects, such as new highways and the like. On these occasions, governments simply take over such property and provide "just compensation." The assumption is that public use trumps private ownership. But not surprisingly, few ousted owners leap at the balm of "just compensation" and go gently into the night. Many resist with every legal weapon they can find.

That's what happened in New London, Connecticut, a depressed coastal city with a grim history of dwindling jobs and a shrinking population. In 2000, New London launched a big plan to revive its economy and expand its tax base. The bait was a $300 million research center owned by the Pfizer pharmaceutical company. The city set out to surround the Pfizer center with money-attracting benefits, including new condominium housing units, more office space, a luxury hotel, and a riverfront park. The plan called for private land developers to lease and build all this on what seemed like an easily acquirable site—a fading Victorian neighborhood called Fort Trumbull, mainly occupied by middle-income homeowners who were expected to love the city's buyout offer.

On the contrary, when the city condemned the property in 2000, the citizens of Fort Trumbull rebelled and refused to take the city's money. The owners of fifteen houses were particularly incensed. They included one woman who had lived in her home for the past eighty-seven years, beginning on the day she was born. Others were young people with scant money, such as an unmarried nurse who had been delighted to find a cottage she could afford.

Represented by a public-interest law firm, the Fort Trumbull homeowners sued the city in state court. They argued that using eminent domain is unconstitutional when government essentially confiscates private property for private purposes, as opposed to public use in the customary sense (a new bridge, say). The city, of course, argued that its entire purpose was public—helping the city bring in more jobs and revenue.

In 2004, the Connecticut Supreme Court upheld New London's use of eminent domain in this particular case. But other courts had sided with a rising tide of protest against eminent domain abuse. Nine state supreme courts had already banned New London–style property condemnations. Accordingly, the fifteen New London homeowners appealed to the U.S. Supreme Court, expecting a sympathetic hearing from a combined majority of both liberal and conservative justices.

It was not to be. By a close vote of five to four, the court instead upheld the city in what conservatives saw as America's biggest blow ever to private property rights—and its biggest boon to governments in league with real-estate developers. Writing for the majority, Justice John Paul Stevens held that New London's redevelopment plan was comprehensive and "carefully formulated" by local officials versed in "discerning local public needs" and thus "entitled to our deference." All in all, Justice Stevens wrote, the city plan clearly served a "public purpose," albeit one beneficial to private developers. In sum, the public-purpose standard carved out by Justice Stevens is now the law of the land, superseding the traditional interpretation of "public use" in the Fifth Amendment.

The four dissenting justices were appalled. Writing for them, Justice Sandra Day O'Connor described the majority reasoning as a kind of reverse Robin Hoodism, empowering government to take from the poor and give to the rich. "Under the banner of economic development," she protested, "all private property is now vulnerable to being taken and transferred to another private owner, so long as it might be upgraded. . . . The specter of condemnation hangs over all property. Nothing is to prevent the state from replacing any Motel 6 with a Ritz-Carlton, any home with a shopping mall, any farm with a factory. . . . The government now has license to transfer property from those with fewer resources to those with more. The Founders cannot have intended this perverse result."

In this extraordinary victory for the country's big shooters—unrestrained bureaucrats, real-estate developers, corporate lobbyists, influence peddlers, with their collaborating legislators and local officials—the losers were citizens with small houses in unfashionable neighborhoods doomed to make way for profiteers masquerading as the avant-garde of progress. *Kelo v. City of New London* tells us that the Court's liberal majority has apparently lost its commitment to a basic American principle—restraining undue government power—and may have lost its human feeling as well.

This case has appalled citizens everywhere—and justly so, for two reasons. First, property rights are fundamental to our free society. As noted conservative philosopher Russell Kirk said, "Freedom and property are closely linked: separate property from private possession, and Leviathan becomes master of all. Upon the foundation of private property, great civilizations are built. The more widespread is the possession of private property, the more stable and productive is a commonwealth."

Property rights have not been respected in all societies, of course, because, as Trotsky and Lenin understood, if the state owns the means of production, dissent leads to starvation. But America and all of Western civilization have viewed property differently. For hundreds of years, private property has been the common people's defense against the state: Within the boundaries of that property, an individual has been his or her own master; however modest the home, the person has a rightful claim to it.

The second reason the *Kelo* verdict rightly stirs outrage is related to the legitimate role of the Court in our society. *Kelo* presented a clear-cut example of a situation in which the Court should have stepped in to undo a gross, unconstitutional seizure of power by government. But whereas the Court failed to act when it had constitutional authority to do so, in many other recent cases it has taken unwarranted action.

Opinions differ on many of the complicated issues of the day, and a spirited debate in our political forums is a healthy expression of democratic process. Such debate is what allows opinions to change and consensus to form. But too frequently in recent years, the Court has stepped in and cut off this debate by imposing its personal moral judgments on the rest of the country. Did the framers really intend for a mere nine individuals to settle complicated moral questions?

Take the issue of when life begins or ends. People's opinions on this question are formed by their different religious beliefs, different life experiences, logical thought patterns, scientific understanding, and individual consciences. As Justice Antonin Scalia wrote in a 1990 case, "The point at which life becomes 'worthless,' and the point at which the means necessary to preserve it become 'extraordinary' or 'inappropriate,' are neither set forth in the Constitution nor known to the nine Justices of this Court, any better than they are known to nine people picked at random from the Kansas City phone directory."

When judges go beyond their proper role of simply interpreting what the originators of the Constitution and written law intended, the door is open for them to impose their moral judgments on the rest of society. Americans should have a say in complicated decisions concerning societal values. When laws are passed by the legislature, we the people are represented in the process; when laws are made and imposed by unelected judges, we do not have a say. The latter form of government is an oligarchy, and it's un-American.

Legitimate judicial activity and limited government intervention are always and everywhere preferable, we believe. But when the government does intervene, how can we tell what will really work at the state and local level, and where our federal tax dollars would simply be wasted? In a word, "experience." We can learn from what has gone before—and the rest of this chapter will take a serious look at three case histories: how Wisconsin led the nation in true welfare reform; how the dysfunctional U.S. air-traffic-control system compares with Canada's new model; and some models of what really works in the educational systems of San Antonio, Texas, and New York City.

REFORMING WELFARE IN WISCONSIN

The battle to "end welfare as we know it" began in the mid-1960s and got nowhere for nearly thirty years. The delay was absurd. All Americans—liberals and conservatives alike—wanted to help society's weakest members, but in those days, the only thing the entrenched bureaucracy could think to do was pour more money into a bad approach.

Anyone could see the system's fatal flaw: The more the federal government supported jobless people until they found work, the more those people avoided work. Lifetime entitlement not only sucked the initiative, the self-reliance, and the very life out of its victims—ironically called "beneficiaries"—it also devoured billions of our tax dollars. Yet nothing improved. Year after year, Washington's would-be welfare reformers were confounded by the Capitol's warring ideologues and vested interests. New ideas from conservatives to abolish welfare's perverse incentive structure disappeared into Washington's maw, never to reappear.

The welfare impasse is a vivid example of the federal government's creative sclerosis, its inability to innovate with either speed or imagination. These are the familiar signs of an obese government, larded with bureaucracy, hierarchy, and immobility. Then why, given its handicaps, do we keep importuning this lumpish monolith to solve every problem besetting the United States?

What might be called "federalitis" is a national folly not only because the federal government is inefficient, but also because the beauty of the United States is that we have fifty governments that are far closer to local conditions and real-life solutions than are our isolated, pampered panjandrums inside the Capital Beltway. No matter which party is in power, the federal government is invariably run by people who strive to "sing on the same page." Most fear being caught "off message," much less dissenting. Hence, it is usually pointless to expect them to offer anything but the same old worn-out solutions. By contrast, the states provide fifty laboratories for testing proposed national policies in a great variety of cultures, ranging from Arizona's sunny optimism to Alabama's religiosity; from Wisconsin's civic-mindedness to Wyoming's rugged individualism.

Wisconsin is the laboratory that ultimately ended welfare as we knew it with a radically new system, astonishing both for its humanity and its practicality. The state's experiments began in 1986, years ahead of other states, when Wisconsin's five million residents were dismayed to discover that their relief rolls had grown to three hundred thousand people. Over the next decade, the state launched many reforms designed to nudge adult recipients out of dependency and into work, a two-stage process that began with giving them incentives and training, then required them to find jobs in order to continue receiving aid. Wisconsin's caseload began falling, a remarkable change during a decade when the caseloads in most other states jumped by a third.

In 1997, Wisconsin switched to a one-stage process. To get public aid, new applicants had to show they were already working in some form. The most employable were steered into private jobs; the least employable had to spend forty hours a week in training programs and public-service jobs. At the same time, the state provided unusually generous benefits, including free child and health care for all families living under the poverty line, regardless of whether they got cash aid. Lest that seem overly generous, Wisconsin demanded something for something. State benefits were rigorously conditioned on work, a standard enforced by sharp-eyed case managers hired specifically to make sure all their clients fulfilled their responsibilities on pain of losing state aid.

Wisconsin's carrot-and-stick welfare system would never have taken off without big spending for staff, facilities, and support services. The result, though, was a decrease in caseloads far beyond expectations—in fact, an 80 percent drop, the biggest of any urban state. The consensus is that tough-love welfare paid off in providing people with work that kindled their self-esteem and rewarded all those who stood on their own feet. The system was a triumph of empathy over spending. By getting people off welfare, Wisconsin quit sabotaging a person's resilience and saved millions of tax dollars in the process.

Wisconsin's successful experiment also benefited the entire country, providing evidence that helped Congress reshape federal welfare standards in 1996. The new federal law eliminated the lifetime entitlement to welfare and replaced it with a five-year limit. It also called on states to test work requirements. Welfare rolls throughout the country have since decreased by more than 60 percent. Since passing welfare reform, Congress has voted ten times to temporarily extend the law's provisions. It is time for our legislators to permanently reauthorize an approach that has proven enormously successful. But at this writing, the bill is stuck in Congress, blocked by legislators reluctant to let go of the old-style welfare state and intent on preventing one political party from taking credit for change over the other. We urge Congress to take the high ground, acknowledge the facts, and pass the legislation.

CONTROLLING AIR TRAFFIC IN CANADA

At first glance, it seems obvious that the nation's air-traffic-control system is best managed by the federal government. What could be more interstate than coast-to-coast aviation? But, as we learned from examining the nation's ailing highway system, Washington tends to be a careless steward of the country's infrastructure. And when it comes to ensuring safe, on-time flights for thousands of air passengers every day, the omnipotent government is beyond careless; it's downright sloppy.

The machinery that keeps jetliners from crashing into each other is so outdated that it would not be surprising to find parts of it held together by duct tape. Owned and operated by the Federal Aviation Administration (FAA), the U.S. Air Traffic Control (ATC) system consists of thousands of anxious, overcaffeinated human controllers trying to defeat disaster night and day. Of necessity, the FAA's main safety strategy is to hold down air traffic by ordering longer takeoff delays and greater space between flights. For airlines, already one of the nation's shakiest industries, the cost of these delays is said to be $3 billion a year in fuel and crew time. For passengers, the yearly cost of wasted time is estimated to be several billions more in missed connections, delayed business meetings, and customer backlash against rotten service by airlines that have no control over the delays.

How did the ATC system get so bad? The basic reason is that the federal government set up a monopoly, thus ignoring principles of competition and private initiative. As such, the current system is powerless to act like an efficient, competitive private business. For one thing, the ATC does not have the flexibility to treat its users like customers who willingly pay fair fees for good service. Instead, the airlines that use ATC and other federal services pay fourteen federal taxes, the cost of which they pass on to passengers. Most ATC revenue comes from these taxes. The elusive remainder comes from Congress's annual handouts, accompanied by scoldings that force FAA managers to neglect their jobs while they repeatedly defend themselves before various subcommittees, much like jetliners waiting and waiting to be cleared for takeoff. Further curbing its financial freedom, the ATC is forbidden to borrow in capital markets, a big obstacle to modernizing its equipment.

The logical answer to this problem is to rescue the ATC from its political masters, pay for it with bonds and user fees, and put it in the capable hands of its actual operators—airports, airlines, and pilots, who know what's needed to make air traffic safe and efficient. That is basically what's been done in fourteen other countries, ranging from Australia to Ukraine, most of which have created user-owned companies to handle air-traffic controllers, while retaining government oversight of safety. The results have been dramatic. Flight delays have declined as much as 25 percent (Germany), while efficiency gains have cut user fees by more than 30 percent (New Zealand). Replacing government air-traffic controllers with corporate versions has now become the option of choice for more than 40 percent of the world's air traffic.

By contrast, the United States seems to be stuck in a political bog that prevents any such rational solution. During the 1990s, the Clinton administration managed to ease somewhat the civil-service rules and federal procurement laws that crippled the FAA's hiring and modernization efforts. But, on the flip side, laws passed by Congress that mandate the purchase of unneeded equipment—unneeded, that is, except by the members of Congress who fight for this pork on behalf of big business in their districts and, not coincidentally, support for the members' reelection campaigns—also prevent our nation's air-traffic-control system from working as effectively as it might. In 1995, however, a big effort by the Clinton administration to explore fundamental reform went nowhere. The idea was to switch air-traffic controllers to a new government-owned corporation similar to Amtrak or the U.S. Postal Service. The sticking point was money: The new company was to be entirely user-financed without tax dollars, and it was authorized to borrow in the capital markets.

This approach was generally hailed by airlines, airports, and the air-traffic controllers' union. It was bitterly opposed by general aviation (i.e., business and private aircraft operators), and also by Congress's aviation subcommittees, for the porkish reason that these groups thrive financially and politically under the user-tax system. User taxes are scaled according to aircraft size. Because general aviation consists of smaller planes, their owners pay only 3 percent of user taxes. But because they often need more attention than jetliners, they account for 20 percent of en route ATC services and nearly 60 percent of airport ATC services. Clearly, general aviation saw no reason to give up a virtually free ride. At the same time, the aviation subcommittees saw no reason to risk losing their power over the FAA's budget of nearly $14 billion a year. Result: victory for the status quo.

If we put aside political obstacles, at least momentarily, we can see that sheer reason dictates the case for getting the federal government out of the ATC in this country, nor should we dither about how to do it. The prototype already exists just across our northern border in Canada, where in 1996 the government sold its ATC operations to a new private company, Nav Canada, a not-for-profit enterprise financed entirely by user fees. Nav Canada is the biggest such air-traffic controllers corporation to date, and the first to be solely controlled by its users and operators. It also intersects directly with the U.S. system, making it easy for Americans to see how it works.

Canada began with ATC problems just like our own, notably political micromanagement and stalled modernization due to stringent personnel and purchasing rules. Starting in the early 1990s, reform proposals focused on creating a mixed government-private corporation. But key stakeholders shot down that model on the ground that (like Amtrak) it would be dependent on politicians, regulators, and government handouts, subverting its autonomy and efficiency. All parties concerned, from airlines and unions to business and private aircraft groups, joined in remarkable agreement that a truly entrepreneurial enterprise was the best way to manage Canada's ATC.

The upshot was Nav Canada, a private corporation that bought the government's ATC system for $1.1 billion in 1996.

Is It the Government's Business?

Nav Canada is, of course, a monopoly, but one with ingenious protections against monopoly abuses. Its fifteen-member board of directors represents all ATC users, includes four independent directors, and bars elected officials and government employees from board service. Nav Canada is funded solely by user fees designed only to cover operational costs rather than make a profit. Indeed, Nav Canada is financed entirely by debt rather than equity, and thus has no shareholders for whom it would have to earn profits. Without the need to build profits, the company's users can focus on containing costs, which they pay and have every reason to minimize. With costs under control, this monopoly also obviates the classic rationale that government regulation is needed to protect a monopoly's customers from exploitation. Nav Canada's customers themselves own the monopoly and have no need for government intervention.

Critics of the current U.S. system see it as a dysfunctional, labor-intensive antique run not for the benefit of its major customers (ranging from airlines to passengers), but for certain groups with narrow interests—unionized employees, turf-minded members of Congress, and private aviation players. As beneficiaries of the status quo, these groups presumably prefer government ATC to any privatization that would end their current advantages. By contrast, mainstream aviation experts seem to concur that only privatization will bring about urgently needed improvements. In 2001, for example, all four of the FAA's previous administrators signed a statement backing drastic change: "ATC is a 24-hour-a-day, 7-day-a-week high-tech service business. It should be operated by a separate corporate entity, paid directly by its customers, and directly accountable to its customers for its performance."

Most reform advocates see Nav Canada as the right model for rejuvenating air-traffic control in the United States. But how to extricate our system from government clutches is another matter. Aviation is a maze of competing interests that have to be mollified before the parts can become a whole.

Robert W. Poole Jr. of the Reason Foundation, a longtime transportation policy analyst, has spent years shaping a Canadian-style reform proposal that he hopes all ATC partisans could approve. For example, he believes that opposition by congressional aviation subcommittees can be overcome by a unified call for commercialization by all aviation stakeholders, led by airlines, as happened in Canada. With tottering older lines like Northwest and USAir fighting off low-cost rivals like Jet Blue and Southwest, this country's airlines, though usually wary of one another, would presumably see the wisdom of calling a temporary truce in order to join in pressuring the subcommittees. The latter would perhaps split into two factions initially—turf minders loath to lose their jurisdiction over government-run ATC, and free marketeers reluctant to launch a new, quasi-governmental Amtrak faltering on wings rather than rails.

Hoping to retain their committee power, the turf minders would seek allies in defending the current system. One obvious candidate is the air-traffic controllers' union, which opposed any switch to a for-profit company back when the Clinton administration was trying to pass a reform package. Robert Poole, the reform proponent, initially calculated that the union would warm up to a not-for-profit corporation, the Canadian model, if its members' pay and benefits were clearly protected during and after the transition. But this sensible idea clearly alarmed many of the turf minders in Congress, who talk a good game about limiting the size of government but, in fact, sabotage reduction efforts that erode their power.

In 2004, the Bush administration began applying an Eisenhower-era process aimed at cutting the burgeoning federal payroll by opening government jobs to commercial competition.

Is It the Government's Business?

Building on a Clinton-era law, the Federal Activities Inventory Reform Act, President Bush is requiring federal agencies to identify jobs that could be done just as well (or better) commercially, and open them up to private-sector competition. Protected from competition are those jobs that are "inherently governmental." As of 2001, the government had identified 850,000 such commercial jobs and begun opening them to private-sector competitors. Impressive savings have followed. The federal budget, for example, used to be printed by the Government Printing Office, a venerable monopoly. A few years back, the process was opened up to competition, and while the GPO kept the contract, it cut its costs by a factor of three to four.

By no coincidence, Congress's turf minders have since introduced House and Senate bills reclassifying certain federal jobs as inherently governmental, thus barring them from commercial competition and preserving them as key constituencies for powerful politicians. These federal employees tend to belong to militant unions with significant clout in electing members of Congress. Among them are the ATC system's unionized preflight information people ("flight service station" personnel), who give pilots weather forecasts and the like.

The claim that ATC jobs are inherently governmental is inherently ludicrous. It is clearly on a collision course with the fact that hundreds of nongovernment controllers already work for some 218 privately run ATC towers throughout the United States, to say nothing of the thousands of controllers now manning commercialized ATC systems in twenty-nine other countries. Indeed, the whole thrust of the "inherently governmental" ploy is a rebuke to any efforts to streamline the federal workforce in keeping with the public interest.

Not surprisingly, President Bush has pledged to veto any bill aimed at diluting those efforts. And he may soon get a chance to live up to that pledge. In July 2005, the House voted to overturn a contract the FAA previously awarded Lockheed Martin to consolidate, upgrade, and operate the FAA's flight service station system. Covering 2,500 employees, the contract, which was projected to save $2.2 billion over the next ten years, is one of the few successes the Bush administration has had in this area. Unfortunately, forty-eight Republicans joined Democrats to pass, by a margin of 238–177, an amendment sponsored by Vermont independent Bernie Sanders to undo the competitive contract with Lockheed Martin. Encouragingly, in October 2005, the Senate approved an amendment that would allow the competitive contract for all but the roughly 200 federal employees close to retirement, which was then agreed upon and signed into law. We the people should demand that our elected representatives support this type of common sense effort to save money by allowing jobs like these to be filled on a competitive basis throughout the federal bureaucracy.

This still leaves the challenge of overcoming the remaining opposition to commercializing air-traffic control in the United States. The believers in real reform in Congress, who want no part of an aerial Amtrak, should be mollified by a U.S. version of Canada's wholly private not-for-profit air-traffic control system, provided all aviation groups support it and it truly removes government from a business better served by market forces.

As for an aviation consensus on a new ATC enterprise, the big question mark is the business and private aircraft operators who comprise the general-aviation category. Given their easy ride under the current system, the private pilots especially worry that a Canadian model would require them to pay user fees based on real costs, thus sharply boosting their cost of flying. Robert Poole's solution begins with guaranteeing general-aviation groups their own two seats on an eleven-member board of stakeholder-directors that also represents air carriers (four seats), airline pilots (one), air-traffic controllers (one), airports (one), and the U.S. government (two). These eleven would elect one director as chief executive and then together choose three independent directors for a total of fifteen—a balance aimed at avoiding airline domination and encouraging all groups to share policymaking, and especially cost control, for the common good.

With two seats on the board, general aviation would be assured a strong voice on policies and would also be expected to contribute a fair share of the company's costs. But what's fair? A complex question given that general-aviation user fees must reflect its actual ATC usage but without crippling its finances and, most important, without tempting some private pilots to forgo weather briefings in order to save money.

Robert Poole offers a simple solution: Charge general-aviation operators for ATC services according to the weight of their aircraft, which vary in size from tiny Piper Cubs to relatively large jetliners. According to Poole's calculations, the owners of a private Falcon 50 weighing 38,800 pounds and making 300 landings a year now pay annual user taxes of $38,812. Under a user-fee system, Poole says, the cost would rise to $57,446, up by $18,634 yet equitable in light of FAA tax and fee reductions. By contrast, the owner of a small Baron private plane weighing 5,400 pounds and making 276 landings a year would see his current user taxes of $1,500 a year become user fees of $2,196, a rise of $696. He and all participants in the new user-run system could also count on their new power to directly control costs and perhaps reduce user fees, a far cry from their nonleverage under big government.

Poole says the government should sell all ATC assets to the new ATC corporation for a net-value price determined by subtracting the old system's electronics from its net book value (including real estate, control towers, etc.). The numbers suggest that the system is worth only $3 to $4 billion, much less than a single year's ATC operating revenue. If so, the purchase price could be easily financed in the capital markets, just as Nav Canada was.

The problem, of course, is that this sensible solution confronts a closing window of opportunity. Given the ever-rising federal deficit and pressure to cut discretionary spending, the chance for government action to modernize this country's dysfunctional air-traffic-control system is waning fast.

SCHOOL REFORM IN NEW YORK AND TEXAS

The Founding Fathers correctly understood that educating our children was a job best left to local control. Indeed, we can be supremely confident that the Founders did not envision a federal role in education. The Northwest Ordinance, passed by the Congress during the summer of 1787, clearly stated that "religion, morality, and knowledge being necessary to good government and the happiness of mankind, schools and means of education shall be encouraged." Yet the Founders later omitted education from Article I, Section 8 of the Constitution, laying out the powers of the federal government. The omission was no accident; the Founders understood the importance of making educational decisions at the local level. It is the right and responsibility of parents, after all, to see to it that their children are inculcated with the proper ethics and values, and given the necessary knowledge and skills to allow them to make their own way in the world. But by taking on an ever-larger role in education, the government has usurped parental rights and responsibilities.

Now, some people are starting to fight back, and one particular uprising threatened to be a potential embarrassment for the Bush administration: Utah, a red-state icon under solid Republican control, was about to become the first state to reject federal control of education under the president's cherished No Child Left Behind Act. So Secretary of Education Margaret Spellings summoned the state's Republican governor, Jon Huntsman Jr., to Washington for a private meeting to convince him to toe the administration's line.

Meanwhile, the equally Republican state legislature had already passed a bill rejecting the No Child Left Behind achievement standards in favor of Utah's own achievement-measurement tests, and the state senate was all set to endorse it. Huntsman, who persuaded the senate to stall, called a special legislative session to reconsider the bill, but the omens weren't good. The state's lawmakers had the votes to pass the bill even over the governor's veto. His talk with Secretary Spellings was called "frank," a diplomatic euphemism for a donnybrook, and he presented President Bush with a letter from Utah's twenty Republican state senators calling the president's attention to the Constitution's Tenth Amendment, which states clearly and straightforwardly that those powers not specifically delegated to the United States nor prohibited to the individual states are reserved to the states. Not mincing words, the letter declared, "Any effective education strategy will respect America's essential historic balance between centralized power and local right."

Clearly, folks in Utah understand one of the nation's firmest traditions: Local education is none of Washington's business. As Representative Margaret Dayton, another Republican, put it crisply to the *Washington Times,* "It is not acceptable for the 6 percent of Utah's education budget which comes from the federal government to control 100 percent of the state's education policy."

The median per-pupil state expenditure was $7,574 in 2002–03, indicating that one-half of the states educated students at a cost of less than $7,574 per student per year. Three states— New Jersey ($12,568), New York ($11,961), and Connecticut ($11,057)—spent more than $11,000 per pupil. The District of

Columbia, which comprises a single urban district, spent $11,847 per pupil. Coincidently, D.C. schools rank among the lowest in school testing, while schools in Utah, the only state to spend less than $5,000 ($4,838) per pupil, rank around the national average or slightly better.

It's clear enough that public education in the United States is a metastasizing disaster. According to the National Assessment of Educational Progress (NAEP), which has been called the nation's report card, fewer than 25 percent of our high school seniors are proficient in math, science, or history. In an international comparison of students in twenty-one countries, U.S. high school seniors ranked eighteenth in math and science literacy. Only about 70 percent of our high school students graduate in four years, and only a third of the graduates have the minimum skills and knowledge needed to enroll in college.

And by most accounts, the federal government's efforts to become involved in education have only contributed to the disaster. A prime example is Head Start, founded in 1965 to benefit preschool children and especially to help poor children overcome the social, educational, and nutritional handicaps that tend to keep them at a permanent disadvantage in schools. The program remains a poster child of the liberal educational establishment, but it has failed to come anywhere near meeting its goals.

In its forty-year history, Head Start has processed more than twenty-one million children; most programs now put children in half-day or full-day classes for eight or nine months a year. But, as The Heritage Foundation's Krista Kafer wrote, "The school readiness gap between poor children and their middle-class peers remains stubbornly large." Low-income children go to kindergarten with a far smaller vocabulary than that of their middle-class peers. "They are also less likely," Kafer says, "to know the letters of the alphabet or even how to follow words left to right across the printed page." And the disadvantage lasts all through school; in NAEP reports, poor students score lower than their peers at all three grade levels tested—fourth, eighth, and twelfth.

Another major federal intervention in education was the 1975 law called the Individuals with Disabilities in Education Act (IDEA). The law was part of a laudable national effort to end discrimination against the disabled, and IDEA has certainly increased their access to public schools. Whether it has improved their education is another matter.

IDEA promised a "free appropriate public education" to all children with disabilities and provided some discretionary federal funding for school districts in establishing programs to meet their special needs. But the law required all public schools to accept all disabled students, to work out special plans for each of them, and to teach them in regular classrooms if their problems didn't make that flat-out impossible.

The main problem is the "individual education plan" schools must prepare for each disabled student, an adversarial haggle that perpetuates disputes, marginalizes parents, and creates a blizzard of paperwork for teachers in the field now euphemistically called "special education." Many children emerge from the process wrongly labeled as "learning disabled," allowing their schools to claim more federal funds. Worse, since the arguing over individualized plans favors children with well-informed, aggressive parents, the benefits tend to go to wealthier children and leave the poor with what's left over.

Besides being an educational disaster, IDEA is a financial calamity. Special education now soaks up $78.3 billion a year, fully 21.4 percent of the $360.2 billion that goes for elementary and secondary public education in the United States. And $6.7 billion of that money goes not for education, but for evaluating and assessing disabled students and creating their individual plans.

Beyond any doubt, local schools could do better—if only they could be left to do it themselves.

Indeed, a report from the Manhattan Institute has demonstrated the effectiveness of charter schools when compared with traditional government-run schools. In a survey of eleven states, charter school students outperformed public school peers on math tests by the equivalent of three percentile points for a student starting at the fiftieth percentile. In Florida, the gain was equal to six percentile points.

If federal intervention in education is a recipe for failure, the good news is that certain local programs succeed, and some are outstanding winners. We'll take an up-close look at two of them—one in New York City's Harlem, the other in San Antonio, Texas.

New York's public schools are currently being run under a schizoid basic policy. On the one hand, Chancellor Joel Klein is centralizing control of the system, stripping power from community school boards, and installing a mandated curriculum that micromanages classroom activity. But at the same time, Klein and Mayor Michael Bloomberg are pushing a pilot program called the "autonomy zone" in which large, unruly schools are being broken up into small ones whose principals can opt out of many of the system's burdensome rules. In return, the autonomy-zone schools agree to be held to strict five-year performance goals, including attendance rates of 90 percent and four-year high school graduation rates of 80 percent—this in a city where less than half of all students graduate in four years.

In largely black and Hispanic central Harlem, Geoffrey Canada has been working for fifteen years to take advantage of just this kind of autonomy. His Harlem Project has set out to prove that all poor kids can succeed in school. He has staked out as his laboratory a sixty-block area of central Harlem that he calls the Harlem Children's Zone. More than 60 percent of its sixty-five hundred youngsters live below the poverty line, and three-fourths of them score below grade level on the state's reading and math tests.

Canada, himself a onetime inner-city child who ran with gangs but went on to Bowdoin College in Maine and the Harvard School of Education, takes a holistic approach to the problem of education. He believes it can work only as part of a program aimed at the whole community. So he sends recruiters door to door to sign up parents and children for programs that begin at birth and follow kids to college, providing an interlocking safety net that aims to keep every child from slipping through.

With financing largely from private donors in the upper echelons of Wall Street, and aided by foundations and a smattering of government money, Canada now has a $24 million annual budget and 650 employees running more than twenty programs. They range from Baby College, aimed at new mothers, to the Employment and Technology Center, where teenagers can hear a Lehman Brothers executive explain how business works and how stocks are bought and sold.

But one way or another, all the programs focus on education, in direct, pragmatic, and, above all, effective ways. At the Harlem Gems preschool program, four-year-olds sit at computer keyboards working on "Hooked on Phonics," with one-on-one teenage tutors coaching over their shoulders. In an after-school program for fifth graders, children write their autobiographies and read them aloud. At Truce, the after-school program for teenagers, a tutor helps an eighth grader with an eight-page research project on the life of Frederick Douglass. And at Madison Avenue and 125th Street, a $44 million building is going up to house Canada's offices and a new charter school, the Promise Academy, which opened in the fall of 2004.

Canada's programs all stress testing to measure achievement and accountability, the notion that progress should be rewarded and failure should have consequences. He aims to find and enroll the kids who need the most help, and then give them what they need to raise their scores. And it works: As Paul Tough reported in *The New York Times Magazine,* when the first set of four-year-olds came to Harlem Gems in 2001, fully 53 percent of them scored "delayed" or "very delayed" on the Bracken Basic Concept Scale for school readiness. By the close of the first year, he had cut that in half; only 26 percent of the children were delayed.

A bit surprisingly, both Mayor Bloomberg and Chancellor Klein are firmly in Geoffrey Canada's corner. Klein has approved his plan to start and expand a charter school in one of the city's public schools, beginning with its kindergarten class, and is encouraging him to convert more traditional public schools to charter schools. Canada wants to expand slowly, but he's eager to begin. As he told the nervous parents at the lottery to pick Promise Academy's first two classes, the promise in its name is simple: "If your child is in our school, we will guarantee that child succeeds. There will be no excuses."

In downtown San Antonio, inner-city kids at the Carver Academy are already reaping the benefits of a similar set of programs. The school—named for the famed botanist George Washington Carver—was founded by David Robinson, the remarkable basketball star of the San Antonio Spurs whose foundation aims to make a lasting impact on his adopted city.

Robinson is a Renaissance man—musician, mathematician, Naval Academy graduate, and ten-time NBA all-star who has been named one of the fifty greatest players in the league's history. His foundation, started with his wife, Valerie, has long had an interest in children. For years, a special block of seats at Spurs home games, known as "Mr. Robinson's neighborhood," has been reserved for underprivileged kids. David and Valerie donated $11 million to jump-start the Carver Academy, and foundations, corporations, and philanthropists across Texas and elsewhere in the country have kicked in another $19 million, enough to finish the first phase of construction of the school and fund some scholarships for low-income students. For his efforts, Robinson was given the prestigious William E. Simon Prize for Philanthropic Leadership.

Carver offers a challenging elementary school program, featuring small classes, leadership opportunities, and a nurturing, family-like environment. And the program is working. On the standardized Stanford Achievement Test, Carver students consistently score in the top 25 percent of all schools tested.

WHAT'S GOING ON HERE?

Highways, aviation, welfare, schools—in each category, the federal government has marched into a vital field of American life, assumed powers not granted to it by the Constitution, presumed that it has all the answers eagerly awaited by a grateful people, and then fallen on its face.

What's going on? The reality that our forefathers knew and that we tend to forget.

Conservatives call it federalism or subsidiarity, meaning that a free society is best guided from its grass roots—from the bottom up, not the top down. As federalists, we aim to keep decision making as close to the people as possible: Do not establish programs so that one rule applies for all local circumstances. Always keep power and control as close to the people as possible. The fact is that some things just aren't Washington's business. When it comes to local highways, airports, poor people, and schoolchildren, the locals invariably know most and the feds know least. But it isn't just the federal government that fails in fields it should avoid. It's any government, city or state, that operates primarily as a bureaucracy. The guiding principle of bureaucracy is to achieve uniformity by compelling individuals to conform in specific categories. By contrast, private or local enterprises flourish by encouraging innovators, creative people, and self-starters with minds of their own—people trying different alternatives to the cookie-cutter pattern of the government system.

What's really going on here, as the next chapter makes clear, is that the United States itself will flourish when we once again truly encourage and honor self-reliance, the jewel in the crown of American values.

THE BOTTOM LINE

- We believe that federal involvement in the lives of American citizens should be minimal, with Washington being the last resort when no other alternative can be found.
- We believe that local solutions are the best solutions in all forms of public activity but particularly in education, transportation, and welfare reform.
- We believe that federal lawmakers and bureaucrats have a tendency to abuse their power in dealing with such policy areas.
- We believe that government bureaucracies are no match for the speed, creativity, and innovation that privately based free marketeers bring to problem solving.

- We believe that judges should simply interpret the law, not make it, and that Americans should have a say in complicated decisions concerning societal values.
- We believe that a free society is best guided from its grass roots, keeping decision making as close to the people as possible.

CHAPTER 3

★ ★ ★ ★ ★ ★ ★ ★ ★ ★

Does It Promote Self-Reliance?

*I predict future happiness for Americans if they can prevent the government from
wasting the labors of the people under the pretense of taking care of them.*

—THOMAS JEFFERSON

THE AMERICAN REPUBLIC was built by the energy and exertions of rugged individualists—pilgrims who crossed the perilous sea in frail ships to brave a wilderness, pioneers who slogged thousands of miles through hostile territory and prevailed against all odds. They had no subsidies, no guarantees, no government help save for raw public land they painfully developed by hard labor. They shared what they had, they helped one another, and they took turns standing guard to protect against danger. They wanted to be free, and they built the freest country in history.

Self-reliance, Tocqueville observed in *Democracy in America*, was the organizing principle of American life, culture, and politics in the nineteenth century. Today, our nation seems to have reversed Tocqueville's admiring formulation and become a nanny state in which more and more individuals depend on government to do not only what they can't do for themselves, but far too much else. Unlike our predecessors, many present-day Americans seemingly do not expect to rely on their own gumption to cope with hardship. Since the 1930s generations have grown up accustomed to depending on the government as their first line of defense against not only real evil but also the common vicissitudes of ordinary life.

Think of the chores we expect our public servants to perform with all the panache of brave first responders tackling a terrorist attack. If you lock your keys inside your car, fail to coax your cat down from a tree, or feel insulted by a surly cabdriver, what do you do? If you're like many milquetoasts in twenty-first-century America, you call 911 and demand action by some hapless fire company or overworked cop, and if you're not satisfied, you may well consult a trial lawyer who will happily file a lawsuit for a hefty contingency fee. Indeed, it is no coincidence that the United States has the most lawyers of any nation on earth. Too often it seems that we Americans love to hire other people to fight even our minor battles while we hold their coats.

Sometimes, these tempests in the American teapot become ludicrous beyond belief, as in the following verbatim call from a citizen to a 911 dispatcher in Orange County, California.

DISPATCHER: Sheriff's department, how can I help you?
CALLER: Yeah, I'm over here at Burger King, right here in San Clemente—
DISPATCHER: Mm-hmm.
CALLER: Um, no, not San Clemente, I'm sorry. Um, I live in San Clemente. I'm in Laguna Niguel, I think that's where I'm at.
DISPATCHER: Uh-huh.
CALLER: I'm at a drive-thru right now.
DISPATCHER: Uh-huh.
CALLER: I ordered my food three times. They're mopping

the floor inside, and I understand they're busy. They're not even busy, okay, I've been the only car here. I asked them four different times to make me a Western Barbecue Burger. Okay, they keep giving me a hamburger with lettuce, tomato, and cheese, onions. And I said, I am not leaving.

DISPATCHER: Uh-huh.

CALLER: I want a Western Burger. Because I just got my kids from tae kwon do; they're hungry. I'm on my way home, and I live in San Clemente.

DISPATCHER: Uh-huh.

CALLER: Okay, she gave me another hamburger. It's wrong. I said four times, I said, "I want it." She goes, "Can you go out and park in front?" I said, "No. I want my hamburger right." So then the lady came to the manager, or whoever she is—she came up and she said, "Um, did you want your money back?" And I said, "No. I want my hamburger. My kids are hungry, and I have to jump on the toll freeway [*sic*]." I said, "I am not leaving this spot," and I said I will call the police, because I want my Western Burger done right. Now is that so hard?

DISPATCHER: Okay, what exactly is it you want us to do for you?

CALLER: Send an officer down here. I want them to make me the right—

DISPATCHER: Ma'am, we're not going to go down there and enforce your Western Bacon Cheeseburger.

CALLER: What am I supposed to do?

DISPATCHER: This is between you and the manager. We're not going to go enforce how to make a hamburger. That's not a criminal issue. There's nothing criminal there.

CALLER: So I just stand here—so I just sit here and block—

DISPATCHER: You need to calmly and rationally speak to the manager and figure out what to do between you.

CALLER: She did come up, and I said, "Can I please have my Western Burger?" She said, "I'm not dealing with it," and she walked away. Because they're mopping the floor, and it's all full of suds, and they don't want to go through there, and—

DISPATCHER: Ma'am, then I suggest you get your money back and go somewhere else. This is not a criminal issue. We can't go out there and make them make you a cheeseburger the way you want it.

CALLER: Well, that is, that—you're supposed to be here to protect me.

DISPATCHER: Well, what are we protecting you from, a wrong cheeseburger?

CALLER: No. It's . . .

DISPATCHER: Is this, like, is this a harmful cheeseburger or something? I don't understand what you want us to do.

CALLER: Well, just come down here! I'm not leaving!

DISPATCHER: No, ma'am, I'm not sending the deputies down there over a cheeseburger! You need to go in there and act like an adult and either get your money back or go home.

CALLER: I do not need to go. She is not acting like an adult herself. I'm sitting here in my car. I just want them to make my kid a Western Burger [unintelligible].

DISPATCHER: Now this is what I suggest: I suggest you get your money back from the manager, and you go on your way home.

CALLER: Okay.

DISPATCHER: Okay? Bye-bye.

CALLER: No . . .

[click]

Does It Promote Self-Reliance?

Footnote: It turns out that Burger King does not now and never has served a Western Bacon Cheeseburger; Carl's Jr. does. It turns out the caller had pulled into the wrong fast-food restaurant. Her tantrum was completely consistent with the behavior of a new class of Americans who deserve a generic name of the type coined by the late, sardonic H. L. Mencken—*boobus crybabyian.*

It's not entirely their fault. The nanny state has conditioned vast numbers of us to view just about any setback as a federal case. If you can't pay your debts, taxes, or tuition; if you can't afford health insurance, rebuild your beach house after a hurricane, or save your business from your own follies, never fear—some federal program will almost certainly bail you out. Moreover, you needn't be poor, friendless, handicapped, or underprivileged to get federal help. The bigger your business and the more egregious your errors, the more you can expect the feds to save you from ruin.

We believe Americans have been sliding into dependency ever since the New Deal began federalizing everyone's life problems, and particularly since Lyndon Johnson launched his so-called Great Society, promising "abundance and liberty for all" via Medicare, Medicaid, the War on Poverty, and so on. What fell by the wayside was the previous American way of dealing with adversity, the era when people in need turned to the civil society all around them, the safety net of families, friends, churches, local doctors, and politicians. People helped one another to help themselves; a network of mutual aid prevailed.

All that changed with the proliferation of federal programs doling out benefits on a colossal scale. Needy people turned to government, becoming dependent on remote bureaucrats disconnected from their lives. Instead of friendship between givers and receivers, the new welfare era fostered distance if not hostility. The needy became bureaucracy's "clients" (rather like "patients"),

59

supplicants filling out forms in search of their tax-paid goodies, now called entitlements. Having become welfare creditors to the debtor government, they next became politically significant, a voting bloc that politicians flirted with and flinched from offending, as in the admonition that Social Security is the "third rail" of American politics—touch it and your career is dead.

Our nation's Declaration of Dependence, so to speak, has affected the American psyche in ways that can and have been charted statistically. Each year, The Heritage Foundation issues a report called the *Index of Dependency* that measures the growth of federal government services in areas that previously were the domain of private, religious, or local communal caregivers. The index focuses on five key areas of typical need—housing, health care and welfare, retirement income, college expenses, and farm subsidies. Starting in 1980 as the baseline, the index shows that, as of 2004, our dependence on federal aid had risen 112 percent, or more than doubled.

The numbers were staggering. Medicare and Medicaid, for example, served 90 million people at a cost of $441 billion, or 20 percent of all federal spending, in 2004. Social Security was ten times more costly than in Lyndon Johnson's time and confronted an awful crunch—middle-aged Americans were losing company pensions and saving so little that half of the entire workforce had no other retirement resources except Social Security, making them solely dependent on the government retirement program just when the number of younger contributors who must pay for their elders had begun declining.

Education was particularly afflicted with dependency. In 2004, roughly two-thirds of all college students got some form of federal help, ranging from grants to loans—and a quarter of undergraduates from families with incomes over $100,000 received financial aid. Perhaps the biggest irony is that all this spending may have actually fueled the relentless rise in college tuitions that bedevils so many students and their parents. Over the past thirty years, Washington has spent $750 billion on financial aid for college students, yet tuition keeps soaring. Why? Heritage dependency researchers believe that every boost in federal aid for students increases their parents' ready cash—providing a kitty that colleges then dip into by raising tuition.

What it all adds up to is a profound loss of the self-reliance and personal responsibility that Tocqueville saw as the prototypical American's core characteristic 170 years ago. As a nation, we have since created the most powerful government on earth. But, all too often, its seemingly benevolent programs succeed only in weakening people and condemning them to endless dependency. Nowhere is this truer than in public housing.

Back in August 1984, Chicago's notorious Robert Taylor Homes were anything but homey. When a newspaper reporter checked out this twelve-story slum—then the world's biggest public-housing project—he found a swill high with the stench of poverty, degradation, and hopelessness. Sewage flooded the court-yards and backed up onto bathroom floors; rats and roaches crawled everywhere. The elevators broke down so often that people preferred to trudge up dark, filthy staircases—havens for drug dealers and muggers—rather than risk getting stuck between floors with little chance of rescue. Playgrounds were deserted because parents didn't want their children so far out of sight. Gangs warred for territory and extracted tribute from the residents.

"When you're up here, you feel trapped," Ethel Marshall told the reporter in her tenth-floor apartment. And trapped was exactly what she was, in a dependency fed by a well-meaning but ultimately destructive set of government programs. She had been there for thirteen years, raising eight children who had been conceived by a succession of fathers. But the rules of the project and the terms of her welfare check forbade any of the men to stay in the apartment, discouraging any long-term relationship that might have led to marriage, independence, and an opportunity to improve her life.

Marshall had dropped out of high school and was untrained for any job. She was rewarded with extra money only for having more children, and she had nowhere else to live if she tried to leave. It was a classic example of Milton Friedman's maxim, "If you want more of something, subsidize it." And now her story was about to be replicated. Her sixteen-year-old daughter was pregnant with her first baby, imprisoning two unwed mothers and three generations of dependency in that grimy, hopeless apartment.

Ethel Marshall's story was so common that the Robert Taylor Homes became a symbol of failure, no better than the slum housing they had been designed to replace. Beginning in the late 1990s, the drab towers came under the wrecking ball, crumbling one by one until, in early 2005, only three of the original twenty-eight buildings still stood.

Surely this dreary denouement forced the project's planners to see the light and rethink their assumptions? Hardly. Like St. Louis's infamous Pruitt-Igoe project, abandoned and blown up in 1972, the Robert Taylor Homes were seen as an architectural failure rather than a disaster of bad public policy. Conventional wisdom had it that the Chicago problem was caused by stuffing poor people into high-rise buildings with insufficient amenities—not by stuffing them into welfare and public-housing programs that inexorably created and nurtured dependency.

Welfare reform has gone a long way toward empowering needy people (more on this topic later), but housing remains stuck in the policies of the past. Failure is endemic in public-housing programs, but their backers don't get the message; they still insist that all would be well if only there were more facilities, or fewer buildings, or different rules. In the past decade, more than

63,000 of the 1.3 million units of public housing have been demolished and another 20,000 are slated to come under the wrecking ball, but the federal government has spent over $5 billion to replace them with newer, more expensive units. All told, some 95,000 units are to be built, of which 48,000 will house displaced former residents.

As a result, the government has supported and even encouraged the proliferation of low-income, single-parent households, with all the social pathology they involve. What's worse, those households and that pathology are concentrated in giant neighborhoods, which become permanent poorhouses that blight entire sections of cities. This effect has been called the "frozen city," and it stands in the way of the natural process of urban renewal that would normally spring up if the projects weren't there. When a project radiates crime, drug dealing, and general despair, what hope can there be for restored houses, small businesses, and lively restaurants and coffee shops that would otherwise pave the way for revitalized neighborhoods?

Home ownership, in sharp contrast to dependence on rent subsidies, truly enables self-reliance. Private property produces pride of ownership. Pride of ownership means people take responsibility to protect, care for, and invest in what is theirs. Government can help or get in the way. Too often, well-intentioned individuals in government enact programs that hinder self-reliance. We must oppose these programs, because they end up hurting the very people they attempt to help.

As usual, Ronald Reagan said it best, in his first inaugural address back in 1981: "It is not my intention to do away with government. It is, rather, to make it work—work with us, not over us; to stand by our side, not ride on our back."

We stand with President Reagan. To that end, this chapter focuses on a central idea: the freedom of the individual to make choices and not depend on government. We hold that a rational view of government for the twenty-first century is one that seeks to promote personal responsibility. We agree with President Bush's words in his second inaugural address: "Self-government relies, in the end, on the governing of the self." And that "edifice of character is built in families, supported by communities with standards," and sustained by "the varied faiths of our people."

Ironically, the principle of self-governance began as the core of what was once liberal thought. A century ago, the thinkers called liberals were committed to the noble ideal of sacrifice, responsibility, ownership, and equality under the law. Then something got lost in translation. As early as 1928, Republican presidential candidate Herbert Hoover observed that liberals had begun calling for more government intervention to curb the economic excesses of the time. In a campaign speech extolling rugged individualism as the source of American prosperity, Hoover chided those liberals (precursors of Franklin Roosevelt's New Dealers) as "illiberals." In his view, "Liberalism should be found not striving to spread bureaucracy but striving to set bounds to it. True liberalism seeks all legitimate freedom, first in the confident belief that without such freedom the pursuit of all other blessings and benefits is vain. That belief is the foundation of all our nation's progress, political as well as economic."

Hoover had the bad luck to say the right thing at the wrong time, but, like him, today's conservatives support the ideas of yesterday's liberals, and, unlike Hoover, we are saying the right thing at the right time. We disown those who hijacked the term "liberal" and then ran amok, using government to solve social problems. Their legacy is a federal budget choked with exploding entitlement programs.

Our country can survive only by reducing what we call the demand side of government—the incessant demands of individuals, of groups such as unions, and of companies that assume that tax dollars exist to finance private causes. We envision a time when people look not to government but to their own savings for pensions, which they will control and can pass on to their children. We see a time when more parents (like most members of Congress) can choose where and how to educate their children, thus improving schools through competition rather than through government spending. The same blessing will come from enlarging access to good private health plans.

We want to end or at least sharply reduce the dependency syndrome that leads people and businesses to expect government help when they should be creating their own solutions. And we want to reduce the addiction of corporations large and small to government favors. If Washington denies tariffs for U.S. steel companies, those corporations will have to compete with foreign imports rather than wail to Congress and the administration. We, as a nation, must stand up against industries raiding the public till, just as Teddy Roosevelt fought giant monopolies a century ago.

And we must also stand up to the so-called public-interest research groups (PIRGs), which spend their time looking for ways to create still more government rules and regulations governing all manner of supposed evils. Under the banner of protecting the environment, encouraging "a fair and sustainable economy," and fostering "a responsive democratic government," these state organizations have lobbied for safe toy laws, "tooth fairy" laws creating public dental programs, bottle-recycling laws, new-car lemon laws, art-supply labeling laws, and bank check-holding limits, to name just a few of the literally hundreds of measures put on the books at their behest over the past thirty years.

Ironically, many of these measures end up hurting the very people they're designed to help. Take, for example, a New York initiative on playground safety. Claiming to be lobbying in support of child safety—an idea everybody supports—a PIRG advocated playground regulations with very small safety benefits and harmful unintended consequences for the city's children.

To begin with, New York City emergency-room pediatricians say that most playground injuries have nothing to do with the equipment and could be avoided if parents paid closer attention to their children. Nevertheless, regulations abound—so many, in fact, that child development researchers warned that playgrounds were losing many of their intended educational and recreational benefits. In the words of Professor Roger Hart, an environmental psychologist at the City University of New York Graduate Center, "[Playgrounds] are basically about running, jumping, and swinging—well, not swinging because that's not allowed anymore—it's more like chimpanzee play." The PIRGs have already removed sandboxes and seesaws from many of our nation's playgrounds, citing fears about bacteria and children's self-esteem (seesaws, you see, allow big children to hold smaller children up in the air). Children, meanwhile, are being denied the opportunity to use their imaginations by manipulating sand into sand castles, or to learn the importance of teamwork and cooperation by moving up and down on their end of a seesaw.

We believe that nearly every government program should be judged by a simple test: Does it promote self-reliance? Does it help make people strong, independent, and useful to themselves, their families, and their communities? Let's take a look at what many consider the three best federal programs ever passed—programs that rewarded performance and were not simply handouts.

The Homestead Act

Once upon a time, the young American republic grew so fast that it became literally land-poor. When the government bought

Louisiana from France in 1803, it doubled the country's size. When it wrested Texas and California from Mexico in the 1840s, the nation became a continent. But soon the United States faced a paradox of hungry immigrants and unfarmed acres. When Congress tried to give away surplus Western land to small farmers, Southerners objected with quarrels about slavery, leaving the West more or less the biggest vacant lot on earth.

Fortunately, the impasse ended in 1862, when the South, having seceded from the Union, freed Congress to pass, and President Abraham Lincoln to sign, the Homestead Act, one of the most important laws in U.S. history. The Homestead Act invited any U.S. resident aged twenty-one or older (man or woman, citizen or not) to become a then vitally needed farmer at government expense. The applicant paid a mere $18 in filing fees for the opportunity to take over 160 acres of public land and farm it for five years. At that point, if the neighbors vouched for his or her success, the applicant kept the farm permanently as private property, free and clear for passing on to future generations. Applicants could also shorten the whole process to six months if they paid $200 for the land, or $1.25 an acre.

Rarely has a federal program worked so well. The act privatized more than 270 million acres of public land—roughly 422,000 square miles, or 11 percent of today's United States. As George Will once noted, that's an area two and a half times bigger than California, or the size of nineteen other states combined. Today, an estimated ninety-three million Americans are the descendants of settlers who homesteaded their way to independence on federal land.

They came from all walks of life—Civil War veterans, recent immigrants, landless farmers from the East, former slaves, single women with resolve and strength. They shared the challenge of building cabins and barns, turning wilderness into fertile farms, and "proving up" their right to keep this "free land" after years of toil and triumph. The money price of admission was small even then, but the sacrifice and hard work required to win a going farm made the experience a test worthy of astronauts training for space travel. Successful homesteaders received a prized credential, a patent certificate conveying the land from the government to the homesteader. Bearing the president's signature, the patent was typically displayed on a cabin wall as a sign of proud membership in America's royal ranks of landowners.

Compared with most American land laws, which tend to promote shortsighted development, the Homestead Act of 1862 had an amazingly long life—124 years. Two million people used it in their attempts to earn government land. About 783,000 (roughly 40 percent) succeeded, transforming their lives and their country in the process.

Eventually, of course, homesteading began to decrease the supply of prime federal land, and in 1934, the Taylor Grazing Act reserved large areas for established ranchers to let their cattle roam. In 1976, the Land Policy and Management Act repealed the Homestead Act in the forty-eight contiguous states, but it did extend the law for ten more years in vast Alaska, where settlers were still needed.

One who answered the final call was Kenneth Deardorff, a young Californian and Vietnam veteran who, in 1974, filed a homestead claim on eighty acres of land on the Stony River in southwestern Alaska. For the next decade, he and his family subsisted entirely on the fruits of the land. He built all his buildings from white spruce trees logged on the property. As noted in a history compiled by the National Park Service, he fished the river for salmon, hunted moose and other critters for food, and often awoke to find grizzly bears in his front yard. Transportation was limited to a boat or sled dogs. Temperatures often dipped to sixty-five degrees below zero.

True, Ken Deardorff and his family had access to conveniences that early homesteaders never imagined, such as a gas generator, power tools, and a short-wave radio. If need be, they could escape via Alaska's intrepid bush pilots, masters of flying small planes across otherwise impassable wilderness. But the Deardorffs faced all the other ancient challenges of life in harsh places—isolation, forest fires, extreme weather, wild animals. When the November freeze-up hits the Alaskan outback, having a radio isn't much help. You're stuck for the next six months.

The Deardorffs prevailed and their eventual farm added the final chapter to the Homestead Act success story. Though he did not actually receive his patent until 1988, Deardorff had written a footnote in U.S. history that no one could take away from him: Ken Deardorff was officially declared the nation's last homesteader in 2001.

With the Homestead Act, the federal government recognized that it had a responsibility under the Constitution to foster economic growth, and that meant "taming the West" so that America could grow and achieve her potential. The crucial element was how the government addressed this monumental challenge: Rather than fostering reliance on Washington and federal spending programs, the Homestead Act unleashed our ancestors' creative energies by giving ownership of public land to individuals. Through a combination of innovation and sweat equity, they in turn transformed that vast undeveloped land into a prosperous and innovative part of the United States. Successful public policy must tap into the individual's drive to build and achieve. Tragically, too many of our policymakers and pundits over the past seventy years or so have forgotten this vital lesson.

The GI Bill

Back in 1940, the average GI was twenty-six and had ended his education after one year of high school. As World War II began and young Americans donned uniforms by the millions, the enormity of this country's commitment to winning began to raise questions about its postwar obligation to those lucky enough to return.

As committed Americans, we believe our nation must always be grateful for the sacrifices the members of our armed forces make in times of war. A great nation should honor and remember its fallen heroes, and welcome with open arms those returning home. In exchange for their service to the nation, all Americans incur a national debt that can only be paid by the federal government—even if local communities and private institutions also choose to show their gratitude in some way.

The issue has an uneasy history: The country gave generous land grants to veterans of both the Revolutionary War and the Civil War, but it was stingy toward World War I veterans, from whom Congress long withheld promised bonuses. In the Depression year of 1932, a vast "Bonus Army" of angry veterans descended on Washington, demanding their due, only to be roughly dispersed by federal troops commanded by General Douglas MacArthur. It was a national embarrassment that President Franklin D. Roosevelt had no intention of repeating.

In the wartime year of 1944, shortly after the Normandy invasion, President Roosevelt signed the GI Bill of Rights, a multibillion-dollar commitment to provide free college educations and low-cost housing loans to what ultimately amounted to thirteen million returning veterans. But the bill barely made it through Congress. Republicans, in particular, were appalled that veterans would be entitled to $20 a week for fifty-two weeks—in their view, an invitation to sloth likely to spoil the recipients and deter them from getting jobs. Worse, they argued, the bill would only strengthen their bête noire, Roosevelt's New Deal, the apotheosis of socialism and the welfare state. It was probably only because Democrats controlled Congress that the bill ever reached Roosevelt's desk.

Also appalled were the heads of various elite universities. Free college for demobilized GIs struck them as folly, a free pass for barbarian invaders. Harvard's president warned that academe would be overrun with "unqualified people, the most unqualified of this generation." The president of the University of Chicago envisioned waves of "educational hobos" riding the rails coast to coast and mooching on one campus after another.

The bill's detractors were wrong, however. Not only were the elitist fears of Harvard and Chicago misplaced, but the policy was a case of sound federal action. America was correct to show its gratitude to veterans who had risked their lives to save the world from totalitarianism. And while many of our veterans could and would be thanked by society's little platoons—small-town victory parades for local heroes, privately sponsored college scholarships, and such—only the federal government had the wherewithal to equally reward all veterans in the substantial and universal way of the GI Bill of Rights.

Most important, the bill was crafted in a way that empowered our returning veterans to improve their lives. Instead of simply providing them with a benefit that created dependency on government, the bill gave veterans a chance to achieve for themselves the independence and rewards of freedom they had fought to preserve.

Because the pressures of war demanded instant leaders, veterans of every service had learned that hard, smart work earned quick promotion. They had also learned that war is the worst of all ways to waste the best years of one's life. Now, as civilians eager to both move ahead and make up for lost time, a whole generation of Americans seized the previously unthinkable notion of going to college.

Probably never before or since have college students worked harder than the classes of 1946 through 1950. For professors of that era, these young men (mostly) were a unique joy to teach. Off duty, they played hard. In class, they pursued learning with a sober curiosity and passion for answers that remains unequaled in the annals of higher education.

But the GI Bill did far more than turn veterans into doctors, lawyers, and engineers. It launched a social revolution and transformed our entire country's expectations. Within five years after the war had ended, the number of U.S. college graduates had doubled, and college soon replaced high school as the national rite of passage. Moreover, the GI Bill that paid veterans to go to college now gave them low-cost loans to buy houses and start businesses, an opportunity that transformed about twelve million young families from city renters to suburban property owners. Unlike many of their parents, these new middle-class Americans owned homes in suburban settings where their children could attend good schools aimed at preparing them for college.

Not every war veteran prospered as much or as soon as the GI Bill's first recipients. Racial segregation in colleges and housing deprived black Americans from enjoying the fruits of the law for many years. Also, the GI Bill never covered thousands of civilians essential to winning the war—the stateside defense workers, 60 percent of them women, who manned the airplane factories, munitions plants, and shipyards that turned out the materials necessary for victory. Had those women gone to college on the GI Bill instead of being forced out of work at war's end, advancements in women's rights would likely have occurred at least a generation sooner.

That said, the GI Bill—and the self-reliance it wrought—undeniably altered the way Americans live, work, and aspire to better futures for their children. To imagine the United States without the GI Bill is sobering, to say the least. At the end of the day, it has to be judged the most successful piece of social legislation in our nation's history.

A nation cannot stake a claim to greatness if it fails to treat its war veterans with dignity. Americans should be proud of the way we welcomed our "greatest generation" home after it defeated Nazism and fascism. Our soldiers risked their lives and made enormous sacrifices so that all of us might continue to live free. The sacrifice we made in turn by enacting the GI Bill of Rights was a well-deserved reward that gave our national heroes the chance to lift themselves, and their posterity, to a better life.

The Welfare Reform Act

Our final example of admirable legislation that promotes self-reliance is the 1996 Welfare Reform Act, which Bill Clinton vetoed twice before finally signing it the third time it reached his desk. The bill was initiated by conservative Republicans to replace the failed social program known as Aid to Families with Dependent Children (AFDC), a totem of liberal Democrats who were appalled at the very thought of Clinton discarding all their tried (but untrue) assumptions about the right way to help families on welfare. To Clinton's credit, he withstood the pressure and signed the bill into law nonetheless.

The new program—Temporary Assistance to Needy Families (TANF)—was championed by then congressman, now senator Jim Talent, a Republican from Missouri. It was aimed at getting poor parents off welfare and into paying jobs, reducing child poverty, and combating illegitimacy. Humane and rational as these goals seemed to the law's drafters, they appeared cruel and outrageous to Clinton's liberal critics, some of whom quit his administration in protest, and most of whom predicted that TANF would increase poverty, hunger, homelessness, and other social evils, especially among single black mothers and their children.

If ever a bill epitomized the differences between the liberal and conservative visions of appropriate public policy, this one was it. The traditional liberal view saw poor people as having a right to assistance based on need, and welfare was considered a form of government charity that society should provide for as long as the poor person needed it. Moreover, assistance was viewed as a one-way obligation—the people being helped were not required to use that help to become self-reliant. Conservatives, led by Talent and then governors Tommy Thompson (Wisconsin) and John Engler (Michigan), decried the condescension implicit in such a worldview, which sees the poor as little more than masses needing to be taken care of. But the worst thing was its effect on low-income families—generation after generation falling apart and stuck in grinding, demoralizing dependency.

Conservatives do not dispute that government should provide assistance to society's weakest members. Where we part ways with liberals is in our notion of welfare as a two-way street between society as a whole and its individual members. We see welfare as a way society helps the poor to get back on their feet, and in exchange for that assistance, the able-bodied have an obligation to give back by finding a job, getting an education, or becoming self-sufficient in some other way. Conservatives thus view a poor person as not just someone in need of assistance, but as a worthwhile and unique individual who also yearns to become a productive member of society. This view bestows dignity on the poor as Americans who should be given a hand when they stumble, not as members of the dependent masses who will have to be looked after forever.

TANF's supporters won the argument. In the years since

Does It Promote Self-Reliance?

Clinton signed it, the reform law has fueled significant changes in American life. Specifically:

- The poverty rate today is about 1.3 percentage points lower than it was before welfare reform.
- Some 1.8 million fewer children live in poverty.
- The poverty rate for black children is near its historic low.
- Hunger among all children is down by over 50 percent.
- Welfare caseloads have decreased by more than half.

The passing of the welfare system as we abhorred it is essentially an old story rediscovered. A welfare system that rewards idleness and irresponsible behavior leads to increases in the need for assistance. By contrast, a welfare system that requires responsibility will draw out the positive energies of recipients, to the benefit of all. Most welfare recipients were able to respond to the new demands of the TANF program in a productive manner. Welfare reform was simply more in tune with the human condition than its doctrinaire critics could bring themselves to imagine. One could suspect that many of the most anti-TANF liberals did not actually trust the people for whom their hearts were conditioned to bleed.

Unfortunately, the continuing hostility of many liberals to TANF has kept the bill in limbo; congressional attempts to reauthorize the program have met with resistance and, as of this writing, are stalled in the Senate.

Moving forward, the focus of debate should be on strengthening welfare reform's most proven positive aspects. The key reform has been to sharply reduce welfare's benefits for nonwork. But more can be done: Congress should make sure that states require all able-bodied adult welfare recipients to seek jobs systematically, upgrade their skills, or do community service in order to receive federal aid. Most important, Congress should recognize that the key to abolishing poverty and welfare dependence is to replace them with the most powerful human institution—stable, productive families. These goals enhance one another: As work requirements increase employment, dependence declines. As incomes rise, parenting and property owning become more feasible. As stable marriages increase, poverty will fade—and children will get the right start for becoming self-sufficient adults.

In our view, autonomy and self-reliance are values Americans should seek and Congress should support with responsible legislation. The lesson of welfare reform is clear: Rewarding idleness, irresponsible behavior, and broken families begets more idleness, more irresponsibility, and more out-of-wedlock children. But rewarding people's innate desire to improve their lot in life and take care of themselves gives them the opportunity to spread their wings and soar toward the stars. This, after all, is what it means to be an American.

THE WAY BACK TO SELF-GOVERNMENT

Throughout this book, we draw a bright line between government programs that promote self-reliance and those that make people dependent. We laud people-empowering as government at its best, and we identify examples, notably the Homestead Act, the GI Bill of Rights, and the Welfare Reform Act of 1996. But those triumphs occurred in the past. Question: What is now America's single best opportunity to match those classics of positive government action?

Answer: fixing Social Security to allow people to control how they wish to live in retirement. No other government action could equal this one for benefiting so many Americans.

Does It Promote Self-Reliance?

The opportunity to achieve true independence for retired Americans has been staring Congress in the face ever since Social Security began in 1935. Yet Congress has persisted in upholding a system that turns most retirees into wards of government, pensioners living on the dole, not people in charge of their own destinies.

Fate has intervened. Social Security as we know it is headed for a crash, presenting us with an enormous opportunity to re-create it as the liberating system for individual autonomy that it should have been all along.

To appreciate what's at stake, you need to know that Social Security has lived on financial fantasies from birth. All the talk about a "trust fund" and a "lockbox" is fiction. The cash you pay in today doesn't build up, awaiting your retirement tomorrow. Instead, it is used immediately to pay yesterday's retirees; you will never see a penny of it. As Nobel Prize–winning MIT economist Paul Samuelson noted, it is similar to the pyramid scheme created by the Boston con man Charles Ponzi in 1920, when he paid some suckers part of what he milked from others while keeping the difference.

In the Social Security pyramid, the system long enjoyed a huge cash surplus because the number of active workers paying in was far larger than the number of retirees being subsidized. But the surplus wasn't saved for the workers. It was scooped up by the U.S. Treasury and used to finance government programs that had nothing to do with Social Security. The fiction here was that the Treasury called this maneuver "borrowing" in return for which it provided collateral—special Treasury bonds (unmarketable anywhere) promising to pay the surplus cash back to the Social Security system. These bonds, actually IOUs, comprised the "trust fund," the only hitch being that the cash to pay future benefits was gone. Of course, the Treasury could borrow elsewhere to pay it back if need be, except that the United States was fast racking up the world's biggest deficit, and enlarging the deficit to benefit retirees just made the problem worse.

The pyramid worked just fine for decades. As long as the workforce grew faster than the retiring population, there would be enough money to go around. So said all the rationalizers who assumed that Social Security would thrive forever.

It was a dubious argument even then, when contributions were flooding in and benefits were still a trickle. Now, with the huge bulge of baby boomers about to burst out of the pipeline into retirement, the game has turned around. As recently as 1980, there were four workers' contributions to support every retiree. By 2030, there will be just two. Depending on who's calculating, Social Security will start paying out more than it takes in around 2017 and will be flat out of reserves by 2041—a slow-motion train wreck happening while we watch.

In reality, the train could crash a good deal sooner than that. The huge Social Security surpluses of recent years have become Treasury windfalls used to pay current general expenses at the rate of some $100 billion annually. Put another way, if it weren't for the Social Security surplus, fiscal 2004's budget deficit of $412 billion would have been over $500 billion, and the added red ink would have had to be soaked up by borrowing or levying additional taxes. In 2017, when the Social Security Trust Fund has to start paying out more than it receives, the Treasury will no longer have the windfall. Moreover, it will have to start raising even more money to pay off the bonds that the trust fund will have to begin cashing out to pay the boomers' pensions. The strain—and the pain—will be excruciating.

Social Security has been helpful for the country. It has saved millions of workers from the disaster of disability and has been the foundation for years of dignified retirement for millions; indeed, for retirees without savings or pensions from their employers, Social Security may provide their only income. The program was also a brilliant political idea, winning national support by including not just low-income workers, but middle- and high-income workers as well, and calling the benefits earned income. "Tell me again," asked Franklin D. Roosevelt as he signed the bill into law. "This isn't welfare, right?"

Even if the Social Security system were fully solvent, there's an added problem no one talks about: It is increasingly shortchanging its beneficiaries. When Social Security began, the payroll tax was just 2 percent of income. Now it's 12.4 percent. Today, the average male worker about to retire will typically get just a 1.27 percent return on his lifetime of taxes—much less than he would get from a savings account. That's bad enough, but the younger you are, the worse it gets. Twenty-five-year-old workers can expect a return of minus 0.64 percent—they actually lose money. Imagine what Congress would say if a private company were taking in billions of dollars from millions of working Americans, and then giving them back less money in retirement.

The ever-bigger bite of payroll taxes on paychecks does even more serious economic damage: Lower-income working Americans have less and less money left to save. It's not surprising that savings have plummeted among lower-income groups. That's a big reason why there's so little investment in low-income neighborhoods. The system needs changing so that more money is saved and stays in these communities.

Even worse, as Heritage's Stuart Butler has noted, "many people pay taxes all their lives and get literally nothing." Because Social Security is only an annuity system paying monthly checks, those with the lowest life expectancy receive the least back. That's particularly bad news for African American men, who, "on average," die younger than whites and so get shortchanged. And if they die before retirement (which, according to the actuarial tables, is all too common), in many circumstances what they've paid into the system is lost to their heirs.

The need for change is urgent, and delay serves no productive end. Indeed, the longer we wait, the worse the system will be for younger generations. Take, for example, a thirty-five-year-old male married to a thirty-year-old woman, each earning around $50,000 a year. Using the Bush Social Security reform proposal as a model, The Heritage Foundation estimates that, for every month that goes by without reform, this couple misses out on $608 that could have gone into their personal retirement account. In other words, the money they lose every month the Congress delays would be more than enough to finance a vacation in retirement or a visit to their grandchildren perhaps.

But the biggest problem with the Social Security system goes far beyond accounting issues or dollars-and-cents returns. It is the issue of individual responsibility and the personal dignity that comes when people have more control over their own lives. As it is, Congress controls the system; you and I have no say over how much we save in it, when we may retire, or how much we will get in our pensions. We have no ownership of our own money, no say in how it will be invested, and no chance to pass it on to our heirs. Far from being empowered, we go hat in hand, depending on Congress to decide how much of the money we've already contributed will be doled out to us. This is the major mistake that has been built into Social Security from the beginning.

As of this writing, the future of Social Security is so mired in political maneuvering for the next election that once aspiring reformers in Congress have seemingly sidelined the issue and become otherwise engaged. This is like the citizens of San Francisco deciding that its next earthquake will never happen because it did not happen today. In fact, the Social Security earthquake is inevitable, assuming our lawmakers avoid pain and do nothing to prevent it.

We ourselves trust the voters to sound the alarm in time to

wake up Congress. At some point soon, there really must be honest debate about such ideas as the personal retirement accounts that President Bush has proposed to reform the Social Security system.

In the meantime, we urge Americans themselves to begin personally debating the most crucial issue of all. Just what kind of Social Security system is best for Americans, not only financially but also morally? We have two possible choices. We can continue the familiar, easy way of the aging pensioner, happily receiving a federal check every month without giving it a thought. Or, we can manage our own money, with minimal help from the government, thus proving that we're still quite capable of managing ourselves, thank you very much. We are pretty sure which choice is best for the American character. What is best for your own character—and pleasure—is a choice only you can make.

BACK TO THE VISION OF THE FOUNDERS

The self-reliance that Tocqueville so admired in Americans is precisely the trait that enabled dispossessed immigrants to master a wilderness and eventually turn it into the world's only superpower. But the phenomenon of our country's success and exceptionalism has come at a price more onerous year by year. Driven by one national emergency after another—from depression to terrorism, from isolation to intervention, from the Civil War to the Iraqi liberation—we have willy-nilly grown a national government that increasingly erodes our self-reliant national character. Vast, prodigal, and pervasive, the federal juggernaut dwarfs our fifty states, devours ever-larger chunks of our taxes, and often demeans the personal independence that our country's founders valued above all else. We have won the world—and perhaps lost ourselves.

This is not the time to even imagine an American withdrawal from the global commitments that leave so much of the world inextricably dependent on this nation's strength and security. But it is time to launch an all-out campaign to reduce the enormous size and scope of the federal government, with its ever-spreading tentacles of dependency throughout American life.

Is this just another impossible dream? Has government so taken on a life of its own that it can't be curbed?

We don't think so. Governments are human inventions, inextricably linked to the moral character of their inventors, the rulers and the ruled. In our case, government of the people, by the people, and for the people, as Abraham Lincoln so eloquently put it, is clearly shaped by the character Americans choose to assume. We can choose freedom or dependence, self-reliance or wardship. We can forget the Founders' vision or revive it. We can take charge of government again by taking charge of ourselves.

THE BOTTOM LINE

- Americans have become victims of the nanny state, dependent upon government to solve virtually every one of life's problems—from debt, taxes, and tuition to self-imposed business failures and the vagaries of Mother Nature.
- Individual freedom and self-reliance must be promoted in order to wean ourselves from the government trough; our country's very survival depends on reducing the demand

side of government, from which individuals, groups, and businesses feel entitled to co-opt every American's tax dollars to finance private causes.

- The traditional public-housing system is a failure. Because private property produces pride of ownership, we should seek to give tenants a stake in the communities in which they live.

- Public policy can be successful—the Homestead Act and the GI Bill prove the point—only when it taps into the individual's drive to build and succeed.

- We do not dispute that government should provide assistance to society's weakest members; but we view welfare as a two-way street of help from society at large in exchange for an individual's determination to become a self-sufficient, productive member of that society.

- Social Security should be revamped to meet our criteria of self-reliance and responsibility, thus drawing out the positive energies of recipients to the benefit of all Americans.

CHAPTER 4

★ ★ ★ ★ ★ ★ ★ ★ ★ ★

Is It Responsible?

If the Congress will not show spending restraint,
I intend to enforce spending restraint.
—PRESIDENT GEORGE W. BUSH

MILLIONS OF AMERICANS APPLAUDED those firm words
in January 2001. In his no-nonsense Texas style, the new president brought to Washington a refreshing air of honesty, realism,
and responsibility. Like Ronald Reagan and other noted conservatives, Bush embraced the country's oldest values—limited government, individual freedom, living within our means. Any
American with a sense of national history heaved a sigh of relief:
We were in good hands.

So where do we now stand?

Item: In the first four years after pledging his presidency to
fiscal responsibility, George W. Bush did not veto a single spending bill. In just his first four years in office, he and Congress raised
discretionary federal outlays by 49 percent, the biggest jump since
World War II. Total federal spending for fiscal year 2006 will be an
estimated $2.6 trillion, an inconceivable sum, twice what it was
only fourteen years ago.

Item: Government gets bigger by the minute. Congress and the administration have expanded Medicare entitlements by creating an $8.7 trillion unfunded liability, begun an unprecedented federal intervention in local public schools, and spent billions on weapons systems that senior Pentagon officials say the country doesn't need.

Item: The total national debt has metastasized. Right after the 2004 election, it reached its legal limit of $7.4 trillion, and Congress had to raise the ceiling by another $800 billion. At the current rate of borrowing, even that limit will likely have to get bumped up again in less than two years. In effect, this debt burdens every American family with an unpaid liability of nearly $100,000. Yet we've only begun to bleed: Since the end of fiscal 2004, the national debt has grown by over $1.6 billion every single day.

As we slide through the beginning of the twenty-first century, one could fairly say: Responsibility is the last priority of most politicians. With honorable exceptions, staying in office takes precedence—and to be fair, short-term officeholders have little chance of making a difference. Too often, clout comes with seniority, and the pressure of always having to worry about the next election is enormous. Going with the flow of their party by doing favors, making deals, and opening doors to power is the easy way out for far too many elected officials in both major political parties. Their idea of responsibility is loyalty to whatever "base" gets them reelected. Too often, that means not individual voters, but big-money special-interest groups. Alas, not enough politicians in either party have consistently shown the backbone to stop the devastating pattern of overspending.

But any government worth keeping is founded on the sacred responsibility of its guardians to defend public safety and expand the greater common good. Which brings us full circle to that ancient question: Who will guard the guardians?

Is It Responsible?

Since governments consist of humans disguised as politicians and masquerading as temporary demigods, they are no more trustworthy than the rest of us. The ways they find to skirt or flout the rules constraining them are ingenious and pervasive. Fecklessness in government comes in four flavors: spending more than the Treasury takes in, wasting the nation's resources, clinging to programs that have outlived their need, and failing to uphold necessary laws already on the books. In this chapter, we will analyze each of these sins. We will also show how this behavior rubs off on all of us, breeding irresponsible citizens in a vicious cycle that could end in the death of freedom. Finally, we will offer some suggestions for forcing our government to behave more responsibly.

IT'S IRRESPONSIBLE TO SPEND WHAT YOU DON'T HAVE

A responsible government lives within its means. True?

Not in Washington, D.C. Not where the biggest squandering machine on earth is beamed to profligate spending round the clock, day or night, rain or shine, Democrats or Republicans in charge.

Yes, the Bush administration has confronted more than its share of superexpensive problems, including terrorism, two wars, a recession, a sinking dollar, a bear market, leaping oil prices, creeping inflation, and unprecedented natural disasters, to list the most obvious. Yet there's no hiding or excusing the fact that federal spending has more than doubled over the past fourteen years, from less than $1.3 trillion per year to an estimated $2.6 trillion in the 2006 federal budget.

There was a time when Republicans accused Democrats of being the party of "tax and spend," but too many of today's Republicans, in their zeal to take on big issues, seem bent on perfecting a new way of operating—*borrow* and spend. The inevitable result is a staggering national debt that threatens the country's financial stability—$7.7 trillion as we write, and rising.

If Lyndon Johnson, back in 1968, had not swept the surpluses in the Social Security Trust Fund into the current budget, the deficit for 2004 would not have been $412 billion, as we were told, but more than $500 billion. And the four annual Clinton budget "surpluses" in the fiscal years 1998–2001, supposedly totaling $558.5 billion, were virtually all the result of raiding the Social Security surplus (to the tune of $557.1 billion).

If, like any company in the nation, the government had to include known future liabilities in its bookkeeping, estimates indicate the national debt would now be reckoned at an astronomical $72 trillion—an incomprehensible number that U.S. comptroller general David Walker calls "chilling."

To be sure, some members of Congress actually try to keep their promises of fiscal restraint. But too many members of Congress remain content to proclaim spending limits and then ignore them. They go on to stuff still more money into already dishonest budgets, concocted by lawmakers who casually grab the nation's money to buy goodies for the voters who keep reelecting them. This mutual back-scratching is not, as its perpetrators regularly boast, one of democracy's noble transactions. It is a crime, even if you won't find many district attorneys willing to prosecute anyone for it.

The Norse god Odin is said to have had a miraculous boar, Sarimner, that provided meat for endless feasting at Valhalla. Each day, Sarimner would be killed and butchered, and the beautiful Valkyrie would serve his pork to Odin's warriors. In the night, Sarimner would come back to life in time for the next day's feast.

Our representatives in Washington have discovered the equivalent of Sarimner: we, the taxpayers. We provide the bottomless barrel of pork for projects large and small that members of Congress wangle for their constituents.

The watchdog group Citizens Against Government Waste publishes an annual study, the *Congressional Pig Book,* documenting this waste of our money. For fiscal 2004, the *Pig Book* lists 10,656 individual projects, each voted by Congress and signed by the president, totaling $22.9 billion in needless government spending. And many of them are dizzyingly irrational. Among the highlights are the following.

Golfing for World Peace

In its wisdom, the Senate added $2 million in fiscal 2004 spending for the First Tee Program in St. Augustine, Florida. First Tee is described on its website as an initiative of the World Golf Foundation, and its focus is to give young people of all backgrounds an opportunity to develop, through golf and character education, life-enhancing values such as honesty, integrity, and sportsmanship. If that isn't worth $2 million of your money, what is?

Jobs for the Irish

The U.S. House of Representatives added $18.5 million for the International Fund for Ireland (IFI), to be spent on "those projects that hold the greatest potential for job creation and equal opportunity for the Irish people." (Never mind that Ireland is now the most prosperous country in Europe.) Projects include producing golf videos, coaching top athletes at a national watersports center, and building a replica of *Jeanie Johnston,* a Canadian ship that ferried victims of the potato famine across the Atlantic Ocean. The IFI is an old friend; since 1986 Congress has given it a total of $439 million for such activities.

Largesse for Largo

As chairman of the House Appropriations Committee, Florida Republican Bill Young made sure his constituents got more than their share of pork. He saw to it, for example, that the Largo police department received $700,000 for laptop computers for its patrol cars. Another $250,000 went to the Pinellas County Police Athletic League. Were these gifts well deserved? Maybe so, but it is irresponsible to force taxpayers in forty-nine other states to pay for them. The federal government doesn't buy computers for all the police cars in Chicago or Los Angeles or even Washington, D.C. It doesn't throw cash at police athletic leagues in Bridgeport, Connecticut, or Mineral Wells, Texas. Those communities pay their own way—unless, of course, they have their own hogs in Congress swilling away at the federal trough.

Public Dollars for Private Causes

Yet another federal pork winner in 2004 was the Rhode Island–based Institute for International Sport, which promotes sport worldwide to "foster friendship and goodwill." The institute stages all sorts of school-age competitions in everything from soccer to spelling bees. It attracts scores of enthusiastic private donors, ranging from Airbus and Merrill Lynch to Wal-Mart and Walt Disney. Even so, it received $100,000 from the U.S. government to fund an approach to combating youth crime. Question: If a private organization is so appealing to private supporters, why is Congress handing it public money?

Is It Responsible?

Buying a Prairie Rain Forest

Ted Townsend, heir to the Townsend meatpacking fortune, decided that Iowa should have what he envisions as the world's biggest enclosed rain forest. According to Citizens Against Government Waste, Townsend has contributed $5 million of his own money toward the eventual cost of $225 million, this for a mere five-acre site where the enclosed trees will need years to grow to rain forest size. Townsend is sure the project will make Iowa a mecca for environmentalists and tourists the world over, and he has lined up some impressive supporters, including former Iowa governor Robert Ray. Flogged by Iowa's Republican senator Charles Grassley, Congress coughed up $50 million in 2004 for the prairie rain-forest-to-be. Stay tuned for more federal aid. By no coincidence, Grassley chairs the Senate Finance Committee.

The Goofy Award

Generations of children around the world have been unable to resist the charms of Walt Disney and his cast of lovable characters. So maybe it's no surprise that a U.S. representative has a soft spot for Disney. When the city of Anaheim, California, home to Uncle Walt's beloved Disneyland, asked its Democratic representative Loretta Sanchez to help give tourists and workers a fun ride around the Disneyland resort and hotels area, Sanchez was only too happy to help. She secured $500,000 in fiscal year 2004 and another $300,000 in 2005 to pay for a bus system to shuttle the Disney folks between venues. Explaining why this appropriation was not pork, Sanchez said, "Tourists from all over the nation and all over the world use it. It alleviates traffic and is environmentally friendly." We think there are better ways to spend $800,000 than on giving Mickey and Minnie a free ride.

Bridges to Nowhere

In Chapter 2, we referred to the now infamous "bridge to no-where" funded in the 2005 highway bill. The proposed bridge—which would rival the Brooklyn Bridge in height, the Golden Gate Bridge in length, and the New York Yankees in cost—would have connected the town of Ketchikan, Alaska, to a small island with only fifty residents. If ever there were a low-priority project for the federal government, this one was it. The irresponsibility of the project was underscored shortly after the highway bill was signed into law when Hurricanes Katrina and Rita devastated the Gulf Coast and destroyed the Twin Spans Bridge over Lake Pontchartrain, which borders New Orleans. Responding to a national outcry, Senator Tom Coburn proposed a commonsense solution—that the federal government live within its means, just as each of us must do in our lives. He suggested the federal government shift the funds allocated to the low-priority Alaskan bridge to financing the unexpected yet urgent task of rebuilding the bridge over Lake Pontchartrain. But common sense has nothing to do with Washington pork-barrel spending, unfortunately: Senator Coburn's proposal was voted down, 15–82. Eventually, after months of public outrage, Congress eliminated this outrageous earmark. Nonetheless, the money allocated for the bridge to nowhere still remained appropriated to Alaska. In short, the responsible step of eliminating low-priority spending to cover an urgent and unexpected priority was ignored. Instead, Congress will pay for rebuilding the bridge over Lake Pontchartrain the politically easy way—by borrowing against our children's future. Well, it is past time for we the people to send a loud and clear message to our representatives: The era of irresponsibility in Washington is over. We demand better!

Is It Responsible?

★ ★ ★

To be sure, all this is relatively minor. The drip-drip of even a thousand such giveaways is less a fiscal danger than a moral outrage. But then we come to the big-ticket items: billions of dollars wasted to support federal agencies that achieve little, and money spent to keep lifeless industries on life support—in sum, to raise irresponsibility to a level not seen since the last Egyptian pharaoh squandered lives and fortunes to immortalize himself in a pile of rock.

To grasp how irresponsibility works in Washington, let's review a simple problem that arose in 2004. Congress rewarded a few industries with export subsidies totaling $5 billion a year, which the World Trade Organization (WTO) ruled illegal. Congress wanted to find a legal way to preserve the benefits. (Of course, these subsidies were inappropriate in the first place, as we will discuss in the next chapter.)

The scent of so much money attracted a swarm of Washington lobbyists with sweet deals. Many of our lawmakers salivated as they rushed to insert unrelated favors for special interests ranging from dog-track owners and bow-and-arrow makers to producers of sonar fish finders. The House produced a bill that would cost $143 billion over ten years; the Senate's even grander version would cost $167 billion—or more than three times the price tag of the original subsidies. The *New York Times* called it "a masterpiece of bad legislation." We call it pitiful.

Under the WTO ruling, the European Union was allowed to levy retaliatory duties on a wide range of U.S. goods. Starting in March 2004, these fees escalated every month that Congress dithered over repealing its illegal subsidies and passing the substitute tax breaks. But the feeding frenzy was so intense that it took lawmakers six months to reconcile the two bills, adding still more special-interest bonanzas in the process. Predictably, the resulting

93

monstrosity was baptized with a false name: "The American Jobs Creation Act of 2004." Among its embarrassments:

- Multinational companies, faced with an incredibly complex U.S. tax code and a corporate tax system that is the 128th worst in the world, tend to keep their overseas profits in foreign bank accounts. An estimated $650 billion now rests in overseas coffers. To lure that money home, the 2004 bill cut the tax rate on overseas profits to 5.25 percent from 35 percent. The U.S. Treasury pegs the cost to the government over the next ten years at $3.3 billion. The blame, however, should go not to the corporations, but to the horribly complex tax system we have in this country. Indeed, the fiscal burden the U.S. government places on our economy is the 108th-heaviest of any country in the world, according to the 2005 Heritage Foundation–*Wall Street Journal Index of Economic Freedom.*

- Roughly eighteen hundred companies benefited from the repealed export subsidy. To replace it, Congress voted to reduce the top tax rate of 35 percent by 3 points, to 32 percent, for manufacturers who engage in "domestic production." That will save some two hundred thousand businesses an estimated $76.5 billion over ten years. And the definition of manufacturing is so flexible, not to say irrational, that it stretches to farmers, software producers, architects, civil engineers, and moviemakers (provided the movies don't include "actual sexually explicit conduct"). As a congressional staffer told the *Wall Street Journal,* "Everybody with a . . . lobbyist is a manufacturer."

The bill's distinctions verge on farce. To fend off Democratic charges that the administration was trying to reclassify hamburger

94

flippers as factory workers, the bill stipulates that profits from meatpacking qualify for the lower tax rate, but profits from selling food at retail outlets are taxed at the full 35 percent. Supermarkets enjoy the reduced rate on earnings from in-house bakeries but must pay the full rate on goods baked elsewhere. And the "Starbucks footnote" explains that roasting beans is manufacturing, but brewing coffee for sale is not.

The 650-page compromise bill was so complex that it came with a 600-page explanation. Even so, many details remained unresolved, awaiting decisions by the secretary of the Treasury—a sure sign that Congress, facing hard choices, had once again punted. The government should save corporations the trouble of finding a lobbyist to give them access to the special-interest tax rate and simply cut the corporate tax rate for everybody.

American taxpayers clearly bear a heavier burden than we should largely because our politicians so often enact senseless measures for motives ranging from the selfish to the self-interested. We're subject to taxation without rationality. It is the thesis of this chapter—indeed of this book—that we must impose reason and responsibility on Washington's irrational political process, and millions of impassioned Americans are the people who can do it.

Right now, too many House and Senate committees have become fiefdoms for endlessly reelected chairmen who fraternize with donors, pressure groups, and special interests, the chief beneficiaries of the laws supposedly being overseen. We the people need to support the opposite kind of chairmen, the heroes of Congress, the right-thinkers who make hard, rational decisions about spending the people's money. These are the stubborn upholders of a unique responsibility: The Constitution (Article I, Section 9, Clause 7) gives Congress the sole power to draw money from the U.S. Treasury for governmental purposes. This power can be abused in myriad ways, but the worst is to sell out to some vested interest and conspire to spend tax dollars for illegitimate purposes. In the past, people have been drawn and quartered for much less, but in today's Washington, with its inscrutable indifference to runaway budgets and inadequately supervised programs, pilfering is a growth industry, captained by a distinct class of buccaneers who specialize in privatizing the public's money.

Consider "earmark," a scam-art term meaning to skim money from an appropriations bill, and then designate it for a pork project that benefits only some tiny coterie of constituents. Needless to say, many politicians see earmarking not in such stark moral terms, but as a quick and efficient way to get funding for worthy projects—and, no doubt, some of the projects so funded are worthwhile. But we revere those who recognize the ugly efflorescence of earmarking in recent years. In 1982, Congress passed a highway bill containing 10 earmarks for pork-barrel goodies—10 too many. By 2005, the number had somehow grown to more than 6,300.

The earmark scandal now appears likely to get a lot worse before the reckoning that surely lies ahead. It turns out that Washington lobbyists have lately begun selling local communities on the notion that earmarks can be engineered for a fee, typically a four-figure monthly retainer. According to a local news report, for example, Virginia's Culpepper County had just begun building a $3.5 million sports complex, funded with voter-approved bonds, when a Washington lobbying group made an offer that was hard to refuse. For $5,000 a month over eighteen months, the lobbyists reportedly claimed, they could persuade Congress to earmark the sports complex, laying its entire $3.5 million cost on Uncle Sam at a county cost of only $90,000. In other words, the lobbyists proposed to sell federal tax money to Culpepper County at a bargain price of only 2.6 cents on the dollar, roughly the current cost of defaulted Argentine bonds. Never mind that they had no right to peddle public money; their assumption that it could be done suggests just how smelly Congress has become. And they were neither wrong nor alone: The market for selling earmarks to hard-pressed communities is apparently thriving and will probably grow, like the medieval sale of indulgences, until our leaders wake up from their current moral snooze and vote it down or face a presidential veto. Yes, Mr. President, you could be our hero.

Of course, the mightiest blow a president could strike for the battered forces of rationality would be to quit cooking the government's books and tell the truth about the state of our government's business. Unlike companies, the government doesn't issue financial reports compiled by steely-eyed auditors using generally accepted accounting principles (GAAP). The government compels all private enterprises to use GAAP and independent certification but excuses itself from doing so. Indeed, it is hard to imagine the U.S. government passing any kind of independent audit.

As a result, we the people have no honest, responsible measure of how much cash is really in the public till. What we have instead is the annual federal budget—a political document designed to make the incumbents look good. You can search the budget in vain for hard facts about the government's actual income and expenses. It is full of soft fictions—pounds and pounds of them—that allow politicians to claim surpluses and hide deficits, whether or not they're real. Let us never forget the hocus-pocus of presidents like Lyndon Johnson, the trickster who caused a huge deficit to disappear by simply diverting Social Security's large surplus into the government's general fund, cutting it off from its previous depository, the Social Security Trust Fund. Such irresponsible manipulations serve only to blind voters and leave our kids unwarned about the debt burden that lies ahead for each of them.

Just like ordinary folks, when governments spend more than they take in, they have to borrow—not for capital expenditures such as homes or education, which would be productive, but just to live and pay interest on their loans. Our government borrows by selling Treasury bills and bonds, and it pays the lenders interest. The interest payments on our enormous national debt now run to more than $350 billion a year, about 17 percent of the government's income.

On the face of it, that may not look so bad. It leaves the vast majority of our income to take care of other needs. But there's another catch: The interest rate we've been paying—less than 5 percent on average—is a record low. Now it has started to rise. As this process continues, we will spend more and more of our federal income to service our debt, leaving less and less to cover discretionary programs like education, national parks, transportation, and the FBI. Interest rates could reach the double-digit level of 1981, but long before that, they would eat up all of the government's annual tax revenues, leaving nothing to spend on any other government activity, from agricultural research to national defense.

Our fiscal irresponsibility exposes us to an even greater danger. Foreign investors now own over 40 percent of our publicly held debt. If the value of the dollar keeps falling, these lenders will inevitably demand higher rates of interest to make up for the reduced value of the bonds they hold when they cash them for euros, pounds, or yen. At some point, foreign lenders may stop buying Treasuries, seeing them as too great a risk. And they might actually start to cash in the Treasuries they hold, driving the bonds' value still lower and rates still higher. At some point, the U.S. government would have no choice but to print the dollars it was unable to borrow, igniting inflation and spinning the whole vicious cycle even faster.

That frightening and all-too-plausible scenario could end

with the American economy in shambles, dragging the world economy down with it. And the whole disaster would be the direct result of fiscal recklessness on the part of our politicians.

IT'S IRRESPONSIBLE TO
WASTE WHAT YOU HAVE

Liberals often scoff at conservative claims that the budget can be balanced by ferreting out waste, fraud, and abuse in government. By their reckoning, no more than $12 billion or so of the budget goes to waste, and while that is not a good thing, it is a tiny fraction of federal spending. But the basic premise of this argument is wrong.

There is far more waste, fraud, and abuse than is generally acknowledged. Congress, however, has largely abandoned its constitutional duty of overseeing the executive branch, and has steadfastly refused to address the waste littered across government programs. Both the House and the Senate have rejected recent moves to come to grips with wasteful spending, and although a small group of House lawmakers have banded together as the Washington Waste Watchers, their cause has not been embraced by enough of their colleagues. One reason is that the legislators see it as a thankless job that would cut into time available for their first priority, which seems to be spending on popular programs and bringing home pork-barrel projects. Another deterrent is that some of the most wasteful programs are also the most popular (including Medicare), and lawmakers fear that they could be branded as "attacking" these programs if they pointed out their flaws.

But there's no shortage of investigative information about waste in government. Literally hundreds of reports are gathering dust in Washington, ranging from studies by the Government Accountability Office (GAO) and the Congressional Budget Office to reports by the inspector general of each federal agency and private think tanks. There is still much to be learned from the Senate Governmental Affairs Committee's 2001 report, *Government at the Brink;* from the 1993–1995 publications of Vice President Al Gore's National Performance Review; and even from the 1984 Grace Commission report on government waste.

The Heritage Foundation's budget expert, Brian Riedl, maintains that a real war on government waste could easily save over $100 billion a year without denting the legitimate benefits of government programs. As a first step, he has identified ten large and small examples of egregious waste that Congress should stamp out, including the following.

Into Thin Air

Buried in the Treasury Department's *2003 Financial Report of the United States Government* is a short section titled, "Unreconciled Transactions Affecting the Change in Net Position." It contains the rather stupefying information that some $24.5 billion of our money vanished into thin air that year. The government knows it was spent by someone, somewhere, on something, but auditors do not know who spent it, where it was spent, or on what. The report says the discrepancy occurred because federal agencies failed to report their expenditures adequately, and it concludes mildly that locating the money is "a priority." It seems unlikely that all of this $24.5 billion was flat-out stolen, but who knows?

Left at the Gate

A recent audit found that the Defense Department had bought, and then failed to use, some 270,000 commercial airline tickets between 1997 and 2003. The tickets were fully refundable, but the Pentagon never bothered to ask for refunds. The cost to the

Is It Responsible?

taxpayers: $100 million. Another $8 million went south when the Pentagon, after buying airline tickets itself, inexplicably paid for them again when employees submitted claims on their expense accounts. (One employee, confronted with seven such false claims, said he hadn't noticed that $9,700 had been paid into his account.) This $108 million could have purchased seven Blackhawk helicopters, seventeen M1 Abrams tanks, or a goodly amount of the body armor that U.S. troops urgently need in Afghanistan and Iraq.

Credit Card Abuse

The government began issuing credit cards to many of its employees as a move to shortcut the hassle of the procurement process. Perhaps inevitably, some government workers have betrayed this trust. At the Department of Agriculture, investigators sampling the records of three hundred workers estimated that 15 percent of all the cardholders had abused their government credit cards, at a cost of $5.8 million. The department promised a thorough investigation, but it will have a huge task: Some 55,000 of its credit cards are in circulation, including 1,549 that are still held, indefensibly, by people who no longer work at the department. A smaller-scale probe at the Defense Department found that over an eighteen-month period, air force and navy personnel used government-funded credit cards to charge at least $102,400 for admission to entertainment events, $48,250 for gambling, $69,300 for cruises, and $73,950 for exotic dance clubs.

Hazardous Waste in Medicare

The Department of Health and Human Services said recently that the Medicare program overspends hugely for drugs and medical equipment and supplies, paying, on average, more than twice what the Department of Veterans Affairs pays for the same items.

Basic payment errors, through fraud or administrative mistakes, cost Medicare $12.3 billion a year, and bills for another $7 billion have gone uncollected. Riedl estimates that Medicare reforms could save $20 billion to $30 billion a year, enough to fund a $3,000 refundable health care tax credit for nearly ten million uninsured low-income households.

Studies in Fraud

In 2002, the Department of Education approved an application for student loan participation by the Y'Hica Institute in London, England. Then the department approved loans for three Y'Hica students and disbursed checks for $55,000. The only problem was that neither the institute nor the students existed; they had all been invented by congressional investigators testing the department's procedures at the behest of Maine's Republican senator Susan Collins. Such carelessness is only part of the reason that federal student loan programs routinely receive poor management reviews from government auditors. At last count, student loans totaling $21.8 billion were in default.

A Dam Shame

The U.S. Army Corps of Engineers spends $5 billion a year building dams and other projects on the nation's waterways. Since it vets its own projects for scientific and economic feasibility, it is often accused of bending its studies to justify harebrained schemes. Investigations by the GAO and several private organizations have found that Corps studies routinely contain dozens of basic arithmetic errors, computer errors, and ridiculous economic assumptions that inflate the benefits of projects by as much as 300 percent. Moreover, the pattern reflects intentional deception, not mere sloppiness. A *Washington Post* investigation found managers ordering analysts to "get creative," to "look for ways to get to yes as fast as possible," and "not to take no for an answer." After a public outcry, the Corps suspended work in 2002 on 150 projects to review the economics used to justify them. But, given the combination of Congress's thirst for pork-barrel projects and the Corps's built-in incentives to approve projects that will increase its budget, its personnel, and its status in Washington, real reforms remain unlikely.

The Medicaid Hemorrhage

Each state runs its own Medicaid program, providing medical care for some forty-four million low-income Americans, and the federal government reimburses the states for an average 57 percent of what the program costs. Thus, the states have an incentive to overreport their spending and, sure enough, they do. Some shuffle money back and forth among state accounts to create an illusion of Medicaid activity; some recover improper Medicaid payments, but then use the money for unrelated programs. Minor reforms passed in 2001 and 2002 are expected to save $70 billion over the next ten years, and Riedl says much larger savings can be had if Congress will take more decisive action.

The Undeserving Poor

The earned income tax credit provides $31 billion in refundable tax credits to nineteen million low-income families. The IRS estimates that $8.5 billion to $9.9 billion of this amount—nearly one-third—is wasted in overpayments. The sheer complexity of calculating the credits is blamed for much of this waste; in addition, fraud and underreporting of income are common, and the IRS lacks the resources to verify the qualifications of all the claimants.

★ ★ ★

And finally, there's another kind of waste going on in government that deserves mention: the waste of human intelligence and common sense. A corollary to irresponsible government action is the failure of government employees to override procedural manuals and take responsible action when common sense dictates. A horror story about a deranged man entering the United States from Canada is a perfect example.

On the morning of April 25, 2005, Gregory Despres, a twenty-two-year-old U.S. citizen carrying a bloody chainsaw, a homemade sword, a hatchet, a knife, and a set of brass knuckles was allowed to walk across the border to Calais, Maine, after telling U.S. Customs officials that he was a Marine who worked for President Bush and that a helicopter was waiting to pick him up.

Later that day, an alert dispatcher in Quincy, Massachusetts, followed up on a bulletin from the Canadian police identifying Despres as "a person of interest" in the decapitation of an elderly Canadian man and the stabbing death of his wife. The bulletin gave a partial Massachusetts driver's license number, and by typing in random extra digits, the dispatcher discovered Despres's Massachusetts address. He was arrested the next day while walking along a highway, dragging a backpack on wheels.

To their credit, the border agents did confiscate Despres's weapons. But why on earth did they allow the man to enter the country in the first place? "Nobody asked us to detain him," said Bill Anthony, a spokesman for U.S. Customs and Border Protection. Noting that Despres was questioned for two hours before being released, Anthony added, "Being bizarre is not a reason to keep somebody out of this country or lock them up. . . . We are governed by laws and regulations, and he did not violate any regulations."

Is It Responsible?

In a tongue-in-cheek column in the *York (Pennsylvania) Daily Record,* Mike Argento, writing in an agent's voice, makes our point: "How were we supposed to know that a bloody chainsaw was dangerous?" the beleaguered agent asks.

Our response would be: by using a little common sense. Border agents should have the authority to use their judgment to make decisions that could be crucial to keeping us safe. Of course, the decisions they make should be reviewed and subject to oversight. We're not lawyers, but if a border patrol agent does not have the authority to keep a deranged man with a bloody chainsaw out of the country, what's the point of having the agent in the first place?

IT'S IRRESPONSIBLE TO FUND UNNECESSARY PROGRAMS

All these specific examples cry out for reform. And there's more. Throughout the government, waste is virtually assured by the overlapping of dozens of programs created over the years to address similar problems. There are, for example, no fewer than 342 separate economic development programs, 130 programs serving the disabled, 130 programs serving at-risk youth, and 90 for early childhood development programs. Hundreds more overlap in other fields, from international trade agencies (17) to teen pregnancy programs (27). The duplication not only wastes time, talent, and money; it also creates a chaotically confusing jumble of standards, rules, and specialty subprograms for potential users to navigate. Clearly, a high priority should be to eliminate many of these programs and consolidate the rest.

Hoarding things that should be thrown away may be a national character trait, as attested by the thousands of ministorage units that dot the landscape across the country. But laziness and plain inertia, however human and understandable, are unforgivable when it comes to the outmoded, unnecessary programs that festoon our government. This kind of waste offers lush opportunities for savings.

The free market is ruthlessly efficient at evaluating products and services, by both rewarding successful providers and forcing failures into bankruptcy and another line of work. Harvard economist Joseph Schumpeter famously called this process "creative destruction," pointing out that a free economy perpetually renews itself as new enterprises sprout from the ruins of the factories that once churned out buggy whips, typewriters, and eight-track tape players.

Appropriately enough, the epitome of creative destruction occurs on Wall Street. The Standard & Poor's 500-stock index was created just thirty-five years ago to provide a yardstick for the stocks of a broad-based swath of large, mature companies in a wide range of industries. Of the original 500 companies in the index, only 78 still exist. Does this mean that investing in the index is a losing proposition? Not at all. If you had put $1,000 a year into the stocks of the S&P 500 for thirty-five years, you would now have $502,000. But companies whose roles became obsolete have gone out of business or merged, to be replaced by healthy firms that compete successfully. The keepers of the index prune it regularly to weed out losers and bring in new winners.

Our government has no such mechanism for destruction and renewal. Instead, Congress has an irresistible impulse to set up at least one program for every problem it has identified, and once a program has been started, it is nearly impossible to get rid of it—even when its problem has long been solved or its approach proven ineffective or duplicative. Any program rapidly develops its own bureaucracy and a set of clients with a vested interest in keeping the program going, come what may. Lawmakers find it much easier to yield to the clamor than to fight for efficiency.

In 1933, for instance, the Tennessee Valley region had been decimated by the Great Depression. Much of its rural population had been sent packing, seeking work in the cities or in the promised land of California. The region had few resources and little infrastructure to support new enterprises. Some argued for the federal government to set up its own corporation, the Tennessee Valley Authority (TVA), to build a chain of dams to generate inexpensive electricity and thus prime the pump for renewal.

The mission has long since been accomplished; the Tennessee Valley is a prosperous, thriving center of industry, agriculture, tourism, and recreation. But the TVA lives on. Now it not only generates and distributes power; it also manages 11,000 miles of shoreline, 420,000 public acres, 54 dams, 14 navigation locks, 1,000 miles of navigable waterway, 174 public recreation areas, 426 miles of trails, 564 miles of roads, and $70 million a year in funds for economic development. Why does one healthy region of the country deserve all these programs at the expense of all the rest of us? Why can't the area fund and coordinate its own initiatives? Why is the federal government still in a power monopoly anyway, when private companies would be happy to buy up the facilities and compete with one another? There are explanations, including inertia, political pressures, and the power of vested interests. But there are no good reasons.

Or how about the Japan-U.S. Friendship Commission? It was created back in 1975 to make grants to promote scholarly, cultural, and artistic activities between Japan and the United States. A trust fund of $18 million was set up to support its activities. Whatever the program's validity may have been then, there's no lack of scholarly, cultural, and artistic interchange between the two countries these days, and a host of private foundations and corporate interests are more than willing to make up any deficiencies. Nevertheless, literally thousands of artists, scholars, musicians, architects, and the like get grants from the fund for junkets to reinforce the two nations' cultural links. If this money were returned to the Treasury, it could surely be used for more important work that now goes unfunded. But any such move would stir up a hornet's nest of outrage among the beneficiaries, so Congress doesn't think the gain would be worth the pain.

Yet another classic example of outdated and needless, but seemingly immortal, government activity is the Rural Utilities Service. It was created during the New Deal as the Rural Electrification Administration to provide jobs and to electrify thinly populated rural areas that private utilities didn't find it profitable to serve. By the 1950s, the percentage of rural homes with electricity matched the percentage in the nation's suburbs. Telephone service was added to the agency's mission in 1949, and rural phone use now tops 99 percent. Because even the agency's managers concede that its services are no longer justified, it is searching again for new missions, such as rural water supply, waste disposal, and broadband and Internet hookups.

Even more wasteful than a program that outlives its problem is one whose problem never existed in the first place. That's the case with the Women's Educational Equity Act, which was passed by Congress in 1974, at the peak of the nation's feminist movement, to promote "equity" in educational policies, programs, activities, and initiatives. It was based on the premise that "teaching and learning practices in the United States are frequently inequitable as such practices relate to women and girls." Over the years, programs created under this act have cost taxpayers a bare minimum of $100 million. Yet according to the GAO, there have been no evaluations of these projects, and thus "little evidence of their effectiveness in eliminating sex bias in education."

In fact, there was never any statistical evidence that any such bias existed, or that girls were damaged by it. Testimony on the bill focused on anecdotal tales of teachers who favored boys and ignored girls when they raised their hands. As Nobel Prize–winning economist George Stigler reminded us: "A string of anecdotes do not constitute data." And if there ever was a gender gap in education, it has long since closed. In 2000, the Education Department surveyed forty-four indicators and concluded that "by most of these measures, females are doing at least as well as males."

If there actually is a gap, it favors girls. As measured by the annual National Assessment of Educational Progress, they do better than boys at all grade levels in reading, writing, languages, civics, and the arts. Girls take more advanced placement courses than boys, are more involved in school activities, have higher rates of graduation at both high school and college levels, and are less likely to participate in high-risk behavior. Boys maintain a slight edge over girls in science and math achievement, but the reading gap favoring girls is three times as large.

Clearly, any program designed to tilt the educational playing field in favor of girls is superfluous. Worse, it wastes money that would be far better used in tackling the real problems of the educational system—chief among them, providing a viable choice to those most disadvantaged by our public school deficiencies.

When President Bush proposed his landmark No Child Left Behind Act in 2001, he designed it to consolidate literally hundreds of educational programs into a few broad categories, giving the states flexible guidelines to use the money where it would do the most good. But all those programs had national constituencies and sponsors in Congress. The House-passed version of the bill authorized forty-seven separate programs, the Senate version kept eighty-nine, and the final bill that went to the president funded forty-five. To nobody's surprise, the Women's Equity Act was among the survivors, and it has weathered every annual bill in the years since.

IT'S IRRESPONSIBLE TO ENCOURAGE LAWBREAKING

America is a nation of immigrants, and these newcomers have kept us strong over the centuries by constantly injecting new doses of the energy and vitality that propel dream seekers to leave for unknown lands. Our success at turning these immigrants into solid American citizens has historically known no equal. But in recent years, huge waves of illegal immigration have threatened to undermine our reverence for the rule of law, creating a serious problem quite apart from the basic debate over whether the influx of immigrants—particularly across our southern border— should be slowed or even stopped. We're talking about the trend toward providing blanket amnesty for illegal aliens instead of returning them to their homelands.

There have always been people who entered the United States illegally or overstayed a visa. But it wasn't until the 1980s that economic woes in Mexico and demand for cheap labor in a booming U.S. economy combined to draw millions of migrants into the United States without the proper authorization. Then, in 1986, a bad precedent was set when the Immigration Reform and Control Act gave effective amnesty to three million illegal residents by offering much quicker legalization with a much lower threshold of requirements.

We believe that it is critical to maintain respect for the rule of law. Amnesty for aliens already on our soil sends the wrong message: It rewards lawbreaking, spurs disrespect for the law, and is unfair to those who play by the rules. If we do not take our laws seriously enough to enforce them, is it surprising that some people feel they are not serious enough to abide by?

To help reverse this dangerous trend, we must expend the

effort, time, and money needed to stop illegal immigration. We must find the manpower and technology necessary to seal our borders, enlisting the help of state and local police in the border states. We should rebuild our tattered Coast Guard, to secure the coast both from illegal migrants and from terrorists.

We must also reduce the incentives that draw illegal migrants to our country. This means continuing the reform of the welfare system to promote self-reliance, family cohesiveness, and financial independence. It also means forcing American employers to bear the full potential cost of any illegal migrants they hire. A bond or insurance system for employers of temporary workers would encourage them to uphold the law and weigh the benefits of hiring against the full costs. If there is really a need for more temporary workers, we should make full use of existing programs to bring them in before we start any new ones.

Incentives for illegal migration can also be reduced by helping Mexico reach greater prosperity and thus reduce the poverty and misery that make migrants desperate enough to risk the journey. This should be done not through direct aid or subsidies, but by encouraging Mexico to promote the internal economic freedom that creates prosperity. Reduced regulation, an end to monopolies and corrupt practices, improved property rights, and freedom of foreign investment could soon give Mexico a strong, stable, free-market economic system. That would provide plenty of opportunity for Mexicans at home—and very probably soak up many of the other Latin Americans who cross Mexico on their way to the United States.

Finally, we must resist any further amnesty, requiring illegal aliens to leave the country and come back legally if they want to become citizens. Our law enforcement should focus first on criminals and those who are evading deportation orders. We must enforce our visa laws and set up mechanisms to make sure legal migrants leave when their visas expire. Nor should businesses be allowed to hire illegal aliens under any circumstances. We need immigrant labor, but we want *legal* immigrant labor.

Enforcing the rule of law is not simply an academic matter. If a law is passed, it must be enforced. Otherwise, it sends the message that the law is not important and a sense of lawlessness is bred. The story of crime in New York City is a perfect case in point.

When Rudolph Giuliani became mayor in 1994, the city was suffering the effects of a subway crime wave that had begun in the late 1980s. Fare beaters, aggressive panhandlers, homeless addicts, and illegal vendors pushing their goods on crowded, already chaotic subway platforms created a disorderly, even threatening atmosphere. So Giuliani, a former prosecutor who had campaigned on a quality-of-life platform, wasted no time in putting William Bratton in charge of the New York Police Department. Bratton refocused a too lenient NYPD on combating petty crime both in the subway and out on the streets; the results proved astounding.

Once New York's finest started paying attention to the small things, crimes of all magnitude began to drop dramatically. The murder rate plunged 39 percent, and the instances of burglary fell by 25 percent. Fewer cars were stolen, fewer people were robbed, and the population at the city morgue plummeted. Mayor Giuliani could proudly proclaim that the Big Apple, so recently feared by out-of-towners and citizens alike, the butt of late-night, unfunny jokes, had become just about the safest large city in America.

What accounted for the NYPD's breathtaking success? It was simple, said the top commanders: The police must take small crimes as seriously as big crimes. It's all part of something called the "Broken Windows Theory," a notion that came to light in 1982 when James Q. Wilson, a political scientist, and George Kelling, a criminologist, wrote about it in the *Atlantic Monthly*. Basically, the idea is that if a broken window in a building is not quickly repaired, other ne'er-do-wells will be emboldened to break more windows, and soon the sense of apathy and neglect will attract hardened criminals, who thrive in such an environment. New York's police force didn't go around repairing windows and picking up trash; instead, they interpreted the Broken Windows Theory as a call to sweep the streets clean of lawbreakers. By refusing to allow drunks, panhandlers, and turnstile jumpers to create disorder in the streets and subways, they sent a message to more dangerous criminals that a crackdown was under way. That and top-notch police work was what it took to halt the crime wave.

GOVERNMENT IRRESPONSIBILITY BREEDS CITIZEN IRRESPONSIBILITY

When our government spends beyond its means, squanders the money it does have, and clings grimly to obsolete programs, its chronic wastefulness is clearly a drag on the economy. If it is allowed to go on long enough, such irresponsibility threatens national prosperity and endangers our country's international prestige and leadership. Perhaps even worse, this behavior erodes the national character that made America what it used to be.

When the government behaves fecklessly, it sends a signal to its citizens that responsibility is out of fashion. It says, in essence, live for today. Don't worry about spending more than you make. Don't bother about saving for your retirement. After all, we need you to spend to the hilt to make the economy grow. Go ahead and run up your credit card debt. Somehow, somewhere, something will get you off the hook. That's the way your government is being run; why should you be any different?

A particularly egregious example occurred after the terrorist attacks of September 11, 2001. With federal funding, New

York State set up a program to aid residents who had been exposed to the toxic dust from the World Trade Center. Washington would provide the cash needed to replace their air conditioners and pay for air purifiers to clean their apartments. Budgeted for $15 million, the program ended up costing $45 million. Why? Because it was structured and administered so carelessly that thousands of New Yorkers who had no legitimate claim to aid were encouraged to apply and get "something for nothing."

A federal audit found that 62 percent of those who received funding weren't eligible, which suggests that about 140,000 people cheated their government. Many lived miles away from Ground Zero, and some had never had an air conditioner. Clearly, they behaved irresponsibly, taking dishonorable advantage of a national tragedy. But as the GAO audit pointed out, federal and state officials invited the fraud when they "reduced managerial controls and increased the risk of abuse." That is another, and more profound, kind of irresponsibility.

When citizens follow the example of government irresponsibility, they feel no need to plan for the future or shepherd the resources they have. As responsibility wanes, opportunism rises. People look for loopholes in the tax law, cheat because "everybody does it," and compete to beggar their neighbors in the conviction that their neighbors don't care for them, either. Time and again, we have seen this process run its course in nations ranging from pre–World War II Italy and Germany to Brazil and Argentina. Government spending runs away as citizens bite ever-larger morsels from the public trough. Deficit spending brings inflation, then hyperinflation, and, finally, financial collapse. Economic ruin ushers in lawlessness, despair, and public disorder. A strongman rises, promising to restore greatness—and he achieves order at the price of civil liberty. Freedom is dead.

We are a long way from that dismal fate. But make no mistake, we are well along the dangerous path. If we don't manage to reverse course, we may find that today is later than we think.

RESTORING RESPONSIBILITY

Luckily, it is not too late to save ourselves and our country. The way to control the federal government is for the American people to demand responsibility, and we have four specific recommendations to bring about this outcome. Once implemented, these measures would not only restore trustworthiness to government, they would encourage citizens to behave more responsibly, too. In brief, we suggest much greater transparency in government; simplified, clear, and much fairer rules for both government and the people; mechanisms that encourage self-control; and the presidential weapon known as the line-item veto. Let's look at them in turn.

Let In the Light

Information is power, and bureaucrats—both in federal agencies and departments and on Capitol Hill in the offices of senators and representatives—guard their turf by keeping secrets. Most government secrets serve no other purpose than turf guarding, but they have the effect of setting up roadblocks to reform, perpetuating outmoded and overlapping programs, and keeping us all in the dark about what our government is really doing. Luckily, technology gives us the means to shine light into the nooks and crannies of the bureaucracy. We must require all government agencies to disclose what they are doing, in clear language, on websites accessible to all comers.

Open information would give citizens the handle they need

to make sure government is honest, efficient, and accountable at all levels, from Food and Drug Administration approvals to Pentagon arms buying, from conflicting Health and Human Services programs to NASA space flights. Let's consider what would happen if we could open up just one major government area, the legislative process.

Suppose it became mandatory that every congressional spending measure and conference report be posted on the Internet for at least one day—twenty-four full hours—before members could vote on it. Technically, that would be simple: Every measure has to be typed up before it can be presented, and the typed document could easily be posted as a file attachment on the Web. That one small step would open the measure to public scrutiny, which (as Nobel laureate F. A. Hayek might have pointed out) is always smarter than any one person.

If you doubt that, ask Dan Rather. In the fall of 2004, his *60 Minutes* broadcast of documents that seemed to prove that President Bush had failed to complete his service in the Texas Air National Guard unraveled under the scrutiny of Internet users. In a brief span of hours, bloggers took the story apart, piece by piece. They noted that the documents were written in a font style common in Microsoft Word, but virtually unheard of when the papers were supposedly written thirty years ago. The bloggers pointed out that the letters in the documents were proportionally spaced, though very few typewriters in the 1970s offered this feature. And they showed that the documents used "superscript" (e.g., making the "th" in 7th smaller and elevated), again, a common feature in Microsoft programs that was unavailable on ordinary typewriters of the day. It might have taken weeks for a single investigator or investigative reporter to uncover all those clues. But through the Web, a typewriter expert here, a graphic designer there, and a computer programmer somewhere else were able to pool their knowledge, examine the documents, and show they were almost surely forgeries—all within hours.

If spending bills were subject to the same scrutiny, Congress might have avoided the goof that forced the House to hold a special session in November 2004. At issue was a $388 billion appropriations measure into which a staff aide had covertly inserted a provision allowing Appropriations Committee staffers to look at the confidential Internal Revenue Service tax records of individuals.

By the time the "mistake" was discovered, House members had already passed the spending bill and gone off on their holiday recess. They had to return to Washington, rework the legislation, and vote again. Had the measure been posted on the Web, individual citizens would have found the dubious clause, talk-radio hosts would have picked up their findings, and voters would have complained to their representatives in time to amend the bill before it came up for final passage.

Such a legislative process would actually be more evolutionary than revolutionary. When Newt Gingrich was Speaker of the House, he helped create "Thomas," which makes every bill available online at thomas.loc.gov. But Thomas doesn't yet include the full text before the bill is voted on. The public ought to be able to comment on measures under consideration. That's a surefire way to make the people more aware and the Congress more accountable.

Make Government Play by the Rules

All too often, citizens confront government regulations that are unclear, contradictory, and camouflaged in legalese as opaque as an old-fashioned mortgage contract. For example, the rules and regulations of the federal income tax code now comprise some nine million words—eleven and a half times more than were needed to create the elegant prose of the King James Bible. Just as businesses have been forced to make their documents intelligible, the government's rules can and should be made far clearer and simpler.

By the same token, government should be held to the same accounting rules that private business has long enforced on itself.

As mentioned earlier, it was Lyndon Johnson who first swept the Social Security Trust Fund into the "unified" federal budget. But every president since, Republican or Democrat, has seized the chance to appropriate the Social Security surplus for the Treasury's general fund. The bonds that the Treasury issues to the trust fund don't count as spending, but the Social Security money goes to reduce the national budget deficit. In the past few years, this has made the deficit look smaller than it actually is by some $200 billion a year.

But that's only part of the shell game the government plays with its accounting. Corporations must take their known future liabilities into account: When they promise to make a payment, it must be recorded as a liability on their books. A major part of the current woes of the big auto companies, for example, is their liability for future pension payments. But the federal government has no such obligation. In 2003, as we mentioned earlier, Congress passed the Medicare prescription drug entitlement. Accounting for an estimated $8.7 trillion of Medicare's staggering seventy-five-year unfunded liability of $29.7 trillion, its costs have been blithely ignored; there is no plan for paying them. As Comptroller General David Walker put it, "There is no way we are going to deliver all the Medicare promises that have been made. No way." But this unfunded liability appears nowhere in the government's accounting. We should hold our government to generally accepted accounting principles. If it's good enough for

Is It Responsible?

Fortune 500 companies, it's good enough for our own federal government.

Government, Control Thyself

Washington needs mechanisms that will help both legislators and bureaucrats control their own worst tendencies. One such reform is to insert a "sunset" clause in every bill creating a new federal agency or program. Such clauses automatically shut down the agency or program after a specified time, unless Congress votes to continue it. This isn't foolproof, since every program develops its vocal constituency. But such a vote would require far more deliberation and reasoning than the annual slipshod debate over increasing a line in the budget for the program or agency.

Back in 1988, Congress invented what could become a model for shutting off wasteful spending that it can't bring itself to stop. The model is called BRAC (Base Realignment and Closing), a system for identifying and shutting down unneeded military bases.

The drive to get rid of our excess military infrastructure has been going on for decades. Secretary of Defense Robert McNamara headed an effort to close bases in the 1960s, and the end of the Vietnam War led to another round of closures in the early 1970s under President Nixon's secretary of defense, Melvin Laird. But it was never easy. Some lawmakers accused the executive branch of using base closing to punish its foes in Congress, and laws were passed forbidding the military to shut down any military base without Congress's consent. In truth, there were too many conflicting political interests to permit a rational way of closing bases in the national interest. No legislator could ever vote to shut down a base in his or her own district.

The BRAC solution was to appoint military and civilian

experts to an arbitration commission, aimed at recommending a package of all the bases that should be closed. Though Congress must approve or reject the commission's recommendations, the package must be voted up or down as a whole. This gives individual lawmakers the political cover they need to act in the national interest, even if bases in their own districts may fall victim to the axe.

It's about time we force Congress to name similar commissions to snuff out wasteful agencies and programs throughout the federal budget.

Bring Back the Line-Item Veto

For generations, presidents have yearned for the power to veto individual spending projects passed, often extraneously, as part of larger bills that can't be vetoed. Republicans made the line-item veto part of their 1980 platform and their 1994 Contract With America, and to everyone's surprise, the measure became law in 1996. President Bill Clinton used it to rule out some $2 billion in pork-barrel spending. But a year later, the Supreme Court ruled the line-item veto unconstitutional on the ground that only Congress has the power to amend money bills after they have passed. The president is authorized only to veto passed bills as a whole.

Since then, presidents have had no choice but to accept all such programs and projects, and they have been proliferating. Increasingly, Congress has been bundling its appropriations into giant catchall bills, each with hundreds of pages of legitimate spending, into which lawmakers stuff projects like sugarplums for their districts. Nobody can be sure of the total amount of pork in the resulting budget, but the 2005 edition of the *Congressional Pig Book* puts the figure at $27.3 billion. The study

Is It Responsible?

counted 13,997 individual pork-barrel projects, an increase of 31 percent over the 2004 total—that's a 31 percent jump in just one year.

Most state governors have line-item vetoes and use them routinely. While the veto is used to partisan effect on occasion, the fear of retaliation serves as a deterrent. When President Clinton had the power, he was accused mainly of using it too sparingly, shaving less than one-tenth of 1 percent from total spending and keeping his hands off projects that benefited powerful lawmakers whose support he needed. A bolder president, however, might make greater use of this handy budget-trimmer—and any use at all would be at least some progress in cutting back the bulging barrel of pork that burdens us now.

A grown-up human being's first duty is to be responsible. That lesson was inescapable in our forefathers' day, when the consequences of feckless behavior were both dire and immediate: The man who failed to weed his garden reaped a meager harvest; the woman who let the porridge burn had hungry children. These days, evading responsibility is too often a kind of sport. In politics, it can be the way to get reelected.

Instead of letting the political class change the subject, we must make them change their ways. But that heyday will never arrive until we the people change our own ways. We must first realize that our representatives go wrong because we let them. We condone; they follow the election returns. We must rediscover in ourselves the commitment to responsibility that guided our forefathers. If they won't behave responsibly, we must throw them out of office and elect people who will. Only then can we devise and deserve truly effective government.

Who will guard our guardians? We must. It's our first duty.

THE BOTTOM LINE

- Government should hold sacred its responsibility to defend public safety and expand the greater common good.
- Out-of-control national debt and hugely expanding government is evidence that responsibility is the last priority of most politicians today.
- A responsible government lives within its means and conserves its resources wherever possible.
- Irresponsible behavior breeds irresponsible citizens, fueling a vicious cycle that threatens freedom.
- We the people must impose reason and responsibility on Washington's irrational political process by demanding greater transparency; clear, simplified, and fair rules and regulations; mechanisms that help legislators and bureaucrats to control their irresponsible impulses; and reinstatement of the presidential line-item veto.
- Leaders who refuse to behave responsibly and meet our demands should be voted out of office and replaced by elected representatives who will.

CHAPTER 5

★ ★ ★ ★ ★ ★ ★ ★ ★ ★

Does It Make America More Prosperous?

Nobody spends somebody else's money as carefully as he spends his own.
Nobody uses somebody else's resources as carefully as he uses his own.
—MILTON FRIEDMAN

To PARAPHRASE MARK TWAIN, everyone talks about the American Dream, but who knows where it comes from? Well, according to author Jeffrey Louis Decker, the words were actually coined in the Depression year of 1931 by James Truslow Adams, a middle-brow historian who tried to use them as the title of his next book. Legend has it, Decker writes, that his editor balked, allegedly saying, "No red-blooded American would pay $3.50 for a dream."

Adams had to settle for *Epic of America,* but his neologism seeped into the public conversation of the time, perhaps because in the wake of the 1929 stock market crash it evoked an image of what millions of Americans had literally just lost and yearned to regain—the dream of individual freedom, homes of their own, money in the bank, and the chance of a better life for their children.

At the core of the dream was, and still is, the promise of a fresh start and future prosperity, assuming the dreamer can muster enough courage, toil, and tenacity to deserve success. For our forefathers, the New World was a land of tremendous opportunity—one where any man could lift himself up to greatness. In old Europe, kings hamstrung their feudal domains with class barriers, state religion, heavy taxes, and regulations that squashed economic growth. By contrast, the United States was all big sky and frontier exuberance, teeming with adventurers, rebels, gamblers, misfits, preachers, sinners, visionaries, and entrepreneurs thirsting to strike it rich. And the young republic, endowed with fabulous resources, protected by two oceans, guided by the first written national constitution, and, hence, the rule of law, enriched by diverse breeds and creeds—with all these ingredients of freedom, the United States earned its own fresh start. By its own account, it was on the way to becoming the world's first classless society.

From this freedom flowed rivers of prosperity, enhanced by technological breakthroughs ranging from the cotton gin to the telegraph and iron railroad tracks. America's business history is full of entrepreneurs who, free to pursue their passions, contributed handsomely without actually intending to. Cyrus McCormick with his reaping machine; Thomas Watson Sr., founder of IBM; and Lloyd Conover, who created the antibiotic tetracycline in the employ of Pfizer—these and many other innovators became wealthy beyond their wildest imaginations, but in fact did a lot more for their countrymen and -women than for themselves.

Sadly, however, America's prosperity is in danger of receding into the past tense. For decades, our government has been promoting the wrong kind of prosperity, usually for the wrong motives and the wrong people. Special interests have gotten the benefits that we pay for through higher prices, tax dollars, and lost jobs. Hobbled by outmoded programs and accumulated layers of regulation, our economy has become less free—and, as other nations see the light and turn to economic freedom, our competitive position in the world is eroding. In our view, government regulation of business should always be effective yet minimal, and it should always err on the side of promoting prosperity for the whole economy and all of our citizens, not just a privileged elite.

On Labor Day 2003, President George Bush announced, "We have a responsibility that when somebody hurts, government has got to move." We disagree because often when government tries to help people in need it crowds out entities that could provide them with better-quality assistance. And further, in its zeal to prevent injury and remedy injustice, our government swims ever deeper in the riptides of overregulation. We have partly ourselves to blame. For too long, Americans have expected government to heal even minor hurts. "There oughta be a law," we cry, and politicians quickly enact yet another curb on our lives.

How does this affect prosperity? All too heavily. The jet engine of prosperity is economic freedom, especially the freedom to take risks. To most of the country's chattering classes—guardians of the news but typically detached from commerce—the role of risk in business is dull stuff, hardly worth reporting. But they miss one gripping drama after another: Behind every great business coup is a huge risk boldly taken. The high-wire daring of nervy entrepreneurs willing to outperform their competitors is absolutely essential to prosperity.

Risk is also essential to living richly, and a nervous-nanny government that tries to overprotect people from risk is a government headed for all sorts of idiocies. A sampling of scaredy-cat warning labels on U.S. products tells the story. There's the blow-dryer admonition: "Do not use while sleeping." Or the food-product caution: "Unwrap before eating." And not least the hand-iron warning: "Never iron clothes on the body."

In a speech at London's University College, British prime

minister Tony Blair laid into the overregulation that plagues his country as well as ours. "We cannot guarantee a risk-free life," he said. Efforts to do so lead only to "a plethora of rules, guidelines, and responses to 'scandals' of one nature or another that ends up having utterly perverse consequences."

Perhaps anticipating a British challenge to the European Union's proposal for statutory audit committees at all companies within the EU, Blair was especially critical of America's own perversity example—Sarbanes-Oxley, the recent federal law that forces CEOs to personally catch crooks in their own companies.

Whisked through Congress in response to the Enron scandal, the law was supposed to protect American investors; instead, it is costing them and us, the stockholders, billions of dollars. For example, the law requires businesses to archive all e-mail (prime evidence for prosecutors), a job that will cost the average large American company $5.1 million a year—every dime of which will be passed on to shareholders and customers. So much for the law's intended "protection" for investors.

As Blair put it in this speech, "There is a delicious irony in this [that] illustrates the unintended consequences of regulation. Sarbanes-Oxley has provided a bonanza for accountants and auditors, the very professions thought to be at fault in the original scandals."

Blair wants to spend a good share of his remaining political capital as prime minister in rolling back the regulatory state, particularly in the EU. He urges far more careful analysis of actual risk and real consequences before government adopts new regulations. "Not every 'scandal' requires a regulatory response," he says.

According to the *Financial Times,* the EU proposal, as originally drafted, would turn voluntary audit regimes like Britain's into something carrying legal responsibility for making sure a company's internal controls, audit, and risk management are keeping operations on the up-and-up. Red tape would proliferate, critics say, and, paradoxically, Britain's high standards of corporate governance might be weakened because qualified people could be deterred from taking nonexecutive directorships.

When an economy is powered by healthy risk taking, volatile yet productive, the resulting competition throws off myriad benefits, ranging from new technologies to higher living standards. Right now, the necessity of being competitive has never been greater. As business becomes increasingly globalized, the economies of the world's nations are increasingly intertwined— because goods are produced and services performed wherever the job can be done most efficiently. This is a good thing for consumers, who benefit from greater choices and lower prices, and for individual workers, who get the opportunity for upward mobility. In reality, as most economists have long agreed, all sides benefit by sticking to what they do best. Let's illustrate that point by comparing two industries in China and the United States.

Let's say American workers can produce either four semiconductors or twelve shirts in an hour, or some combination in between (say, one semiconductor and nine shirts). In China, workers can turn out two semiconductors or ten shirts in an hour. The Americans have an absolute edge in both fields. But the United States is twice as good as China at making semiconductors, and only 1.2 times as good at making shirts. So it has a comparative advantage in semiconductors.

If the two countries don't trade, America might choose to produce (and be able to use) two semiconductors and six shirts for each hour worked. China might choose to have only one semiconductor and five shirts per hour worked. But if the United States produces only semiconductors and trades half its output for shirts from China, it will wind up with two semiconductors, just as before, while it can trade the other two semiconductors for eight shirts—a gain of two shirts. China has lost three shirts, but gained a semiconductor that is worth four shirts. Both sides come out ahead.

As this example shows, international trade—that is, globalization—is not a development that should frighten Americans. For all the hand-wringing in the popular press over the "outsourcing" of production, we can profit from it. Free trade brings enormous benefits to all the partners who can learn the rules and adapt to the new conditions. And in the end, if economic freedom is maintained, outsourcing begets insourcing: Nissan, Subaru, Toyota, and now Hyundai have all opened factories in the United States.

Free trade is an idea that goes back to Adam Smith, the founder of modern economics. It was Smith who first said, "If a foreign country can supply us with a commodity cheaper than we ourselves can make it, better buy it off them"—and pay for it with some good or service that we have the comparative advantage in turning out. This, in fact, is the secret of human progress. In ancient times, some people were more skilled than others at weaving. They specialized in it and were paid for their work with the food that others were better at hunting and gathering—and, eventually, growing. The result was more of everything for everyone, thus providing an early lesson in the efficiency of international trade and specialization, and how it fosters expansion in real wealth for all. International trade yields the same fruits today.

In the past century, advances in farm technology freed millions to work in factories. Now, automation and competition from low-wage nations are displacing industrial workers, thus freeing Americans to concentrate on research and development and the sophisticated services where we maintain a comparative edge. In fact, the loss of two million manufacturing jobs in recent years has been more than made up for by the addition of four million new white-collar jobs—and all the while, American industrial output has still risen as a result of automated processes.

Yes, our nation will lose many more jobs in manufacturing, but it will continue to expand its manufacturing output. The march of progress becomes a tragedy only for those who cannot be retrained for better, higher-value, and more fulfilling work. Even here, America leads the way with retraining programs, vocational and community colleges, and other opportunities for every American to stay in the mainstream. As a nation, we must learn to work with our minds rather than our hands. We must take education and retraining seriously and halt the deterioration of our public schools; we must produce the finest minds in the world and attract the brightest students from abroad to study in our country. And once they are here, we need a fair and sensible immigration policy that allows them to stay.

THE WRONG KIND OF PROSPERITY

Unfortunately, there is a shortage of sensible policy in Washington. From the federal budget and pork-barrel spending to protectionist trade barriers, the federal government, as noted earlier, has been promoting shortsighted policies that produce prosperity for a few at the expense of the rest of us.

In the depths of the Depression, President Franklin D. Roosevelt and Congress were concerned that many farmers were being driven into bankruptcy by plummeting crop prices. So lawmakers passed the New Deal's Agricultural Adjustment Act of 1933. It aimed to boost prices by paying farmers to slash their planting, thus cutting back the surplus crops that hard-pressed Americans weren't buying. The policy worked: Farm prices rose and the crisis eased.

Today, that offer still stands, but to whose benefit? Here's a sampling of the folks who prospered from farm subsidies in recent years:

- David Rockefeller, former chairman and chief executive officer of Chase Manhattan Bank and an heir to the vast Rockefeller fortune, has received $518,122 in farm subsidies from Washington.
- Scottie Pippen, the onetime Chicago Bulls basketball star who was Michael Jordan's sidekick and one of the highest-paid players of all time, has been paid $210,520.
- Ted Turner, Cable News Network founder, media mogul, and number twenty-five on *Forbes* magazine's list of the five hundred wealthiest people in the United States, has been paid $206,948.

Need we ask any American whether these people need help from their government? Of course they don't. The prosperity they enjoy from this policy comes at the expense of everyone else; the tax money spent to make them even wealthier is clearly a waste of resources and a burden on all of us taxpayers and on the entire economy. And to the extent that the giveaway actually produces the original objective—higher prices—it is an even greater economic load, since consumers who must pay them can't spend the money on something else.

Yet federal giveaways to pseudofarmers who don't need them are just minor signs of how truly counterproductive our country's agricultural policies have become. And the farm policies themselves are just tiny blips on the full screen of counterproductive laws, policies, and programs that successive Congresses and administrations of both parties have imposed on us, the people.

When the government first went into the farm-subsidy business, it made sense. We started out as a rural nation, and we needed to encourage our small farmers to produce more and more as the population expanded. Since state and territorial governments lacked resources for the job, it fell to the federal government to meet the need. Over the years, we—via our representatives in Washington—provided farmers with free land, railroads to move their crops, irrigation systems, crop research, and agricultural colleges. We also made low-cost loans available to tide farmers over when disaster, in the form of bad weather or low prices, left them without the cash they needed to buy seed for the next year's crops.

But gradually at first, then in a rush, the small farmer began to disappear. Mechanization and new farming techniques were best suited to larger operations, and wealthy farmers bought out their less successful neighbors. The Depression of the 1930s pushed many farmers to find other work in the big cities. Later, other small farmers sold out to real-estate developers, who built the suburbs that now spread across our nation. Those who held on to their farms found themselves unable to compete against the huge, technologically advanced, superefficient agribusiness operations.

In 1930, nearly one out of four working Americans was a farmer; by 2000, farm workers numbered fewer than one out of one hundred. Farming had become big business. Since 1935 the number of U.S. farms has plummeted from seven million to two million—only four hundred thousand of them full-time operations—while the average farm has grown from 150 acres to more than 500 acres. Clearly, any rational assessment of the need for incentives would have required our lawmakers to reduce or eliminate farm subsidies. But that isn't the logic of Washington politics.

In the years during and after World War II, the farm states lost some thirty-two million residents as small farmers moved into towns and cities to follow their dreams. But the states kept their electoral-college and senatorial clout, which set the stage for the politicians: Farm-bloc lawmakers of both parties joined forces to win ever-bigger subsidies for ever-fewer farmers.

The result was and is a fiscal folly worthy of some great satirist—Charles Dickens, say, or Jonathan Swift. It defies all but political reasoning. For example, as Heritage's Brian Riedl has noted, the budget-busting $180 billion farm bill passed before the 2002 elections actually encourages overproduction, pushing down prices and eroding farm income—reversing the goals of the original subsidies. It also undermines overseas trade and encourages other nations to put up barriers to U.S. exports. But if it harms the economy in general, it does bring prosperity to a favored few: huge corporate farms, a handful of lawmakers sitting on agriculture committees, and celebrities—David Rockefeller et al.—with tax shelters camouflaged as farms.

How did farm subsidies become corporate welfare? Easy: The subsidies have nothing to do with a recipient's income or financial need; they are determined by the crop you choose to raise and its size. Growers of the big-five favored crops—corn, cotton, rice, soybeans, and wheat—receive more than 90 percent of all farm subsidies. Growers of nearly four hundred other domestic crops, Riedl has pointed out, are completely shut out. The more acres you plant of the five preferred crops, the more government subsidies you receive. Size trumps everything else: In 2002, the most recent year for which figures are available, nearly two-thirds of farm subsidies went to a mere 10 percent of all recipients.

Big farms keep on buying up small ones, and the subsidies have fueled the consolidation process. In 2002, corporate farmers received a huge, extra, and irrational bonus. They browbeat Congress into tripling the subsidy giveaway—now $30 billion a year—on the grounds that crop prices had fallen ("dipped a bit" would be a better term), and they needed "emergency" help.

Enhancing the prosperity of corporate farms that don't need taxpayers' money clearly imposes a burden on everyone else in the country. The big winners are often giant companies that practice agriculture at best as a subsidiary or minor division—corporations like John Hancock, which most people would call an insurance company but which, in 2002 alone, got $2,289,364 as a sometime "farm" operator. Other eyebrow-raising beneficiaries that year included nine members of Congress, five of them sitting on committees overseeing U.S. agriculture. They received subsidies averaging forty-six times those given to the country's typical farmer.

The explanation for this folly is that our representatives have recklessly yielded to pressure from special interests, and we the people have done little or nothing to stop them. The farm giveaway is just a single example of that failure.

Wrongheaded as the big-five subsidies are, the poster child of dysfunctional farm benefits has to be the U.S. sugar program, which promotes prosperity for a tiny handful of wealthy growers at enormous expense to the rest of the economy, American diplomatic policy, and much of the third world.

The plain fact is that sugar is not an economically viable crop in the latitudes of the United States. In the tropics, sugarcane grows all but spontaneously and can be harvested and processed with inexpensive labor; sugarcane in Florida, or sugar beets in Minnesota, simply can't compete on a level playing field.

Nevertheless, U.S. sugar growers have enjoyed subsidies of one kind or another ever since the War of 1812. Direct subsidies have been used, but tariffs and import quotas to keep foreign sugar off the American market have been more the style in sugar. In 1816, high tariffs were imposed to placate farmers in the newly acquired Louisiana Territory. At first, the rationale was that the growers needed help until they could compete (an argument, critics wisecrack, that makes sugar the nation's oldest infant industry). Over time, however, the justifications have varied. At one point, protectionists warned that lifting the tariffs would touch off a collapse in the price of slaves, thus undermining the pre–Civil War economy. More recently, import quotas have been defended as a way to guard against "roller-coaster" world price gyrations, or to protect the industry long enough for it to switch to other products—as if it ever would while the subsidies last.

The prosperity created by these distortions of the free market is channeled to a tiny handful of happy citizens. In all, there are only thirteen thousand sugar growers in the United States. And according to Congress's GAO, only seventeen of the largest of them walk off with half of all the rewards. In Florida, a single family, the Fanjuls, is said to get half of all benefits paid in the state, and the twenty-eight largest growers accounted for 90 percent of Florida's booty.

The cost to the rest of us for sugar subsidies is not very sweet. Americans pay as much as seven times the world price for sugar. Each added penny for a pound of sugar raises the nation's food bill by at least $250 million; a Commerce Department study found that the sugar program costs U.S. consumers more than $3 billion a year. And the cost isn't measured in dollars and cents alone. In Minnesota's Red River Valley, as author James Bovard has noted, subsidized sugar growers have bid up the price of land so high that many unsubsidized farmers can't buy more fields. In Louisiana, the sugar industry's uneconomic diversion of resources has been blamed for the state's "brain drain" of educated people looking for opportunities elsewhere.

The sugar program is counterproductive in many ways. When Brazil retaliated for a cut in its sugar quota by restricting purchases of U.S. grain, our wheat and corn exporters suffered. When third world farmers couldn't sell sugar and turned to cultivating marijuana, our import quotas became a full-employment act for the Drug Enforcement Agency. And in 1984, the price of sugar rose so high that it wrecked the market: Coke and Pepsi-Cola both announced that they were replacing sugar with high-fructose corn syrup. Sugar use dropped, Bovard reported, by five hundred thousand tons a year, equivalent to the entire quotas of twenty-five of the forty-two nations permitted to sell sugar to the United States. The government's response: another 20 percent cut in quotas.

Moreover, our beneficence to a few sugar growers has consequences far beyond our shores. Despite Ronald Reagan's promise to help Caribbean nations by giving them freer access to U.S. markets, his administration cut Caribbean sugar quotas by 74 percent over several years, a cut that cost third world producers $800 million a year. To offset the damage, the U.S. government then announced a program to distribute food. In 1986 alone, $200 million worth of free food was dumped in the Caribbean and the Philippines. This drove their domestic commodity prices down and made it even harder for former sugar growers in the poor countries to switch to other crops. "It makes us look like damn fools," Richard Holwell, deputy assistant secretary of state, observed, "when we go down there and preach free enterprise."

The tormented sugar program, with all its distortions and market disruptions, has long since lost any pretense of rationality or respectability. It's clear to anyone who takes more than a cursory glance that everyone except the fraternity of wealthy growers would benefit if sugar were traded on a free market. Yet the sugar lobby prevails.

And the growers get a remarkable bargain in Washington. In the 2004 election cycle, sugar interests made $3.2 million worth of contributions to federal campaigns. That's in addition to $3.1 million in 2002 and $3.4 million in 2004. Incumbents in Congress benefit enormously from big sugar—and we are the ones who pay.

TWELFTH PLACE IS A BAD PLACE

My native land, my joy, delight,
How fair thou art and bright!
And nowhere in the world all round
Can ever such a place be found
So well beloved as I love thee,
My native country dear!

—Opening stanza to the Estonian national anthem

Speaking of the wrong kind of prosperity, it turns out that mighty America has lately become so overregulated as to fall from its once high perch as the world's fourth-freest economy. The new number four titleholder is none other than little Estonia, a proud Baltic survivor, thriving ever since it escaped Soviet rule with its nationhood intact in 1991. Estonia is roughly the size of two New Hampshires and has a population less than 1.5 percent of America's.

The demotion of the United States was recorded in the 2005 annual *Index of Economic Freedom,* published jointly since 1995 by The Heritage Foundation and the *Wall Street Journal.* The index measures economic freedom (different from political freedom) and concludes that the more economic freedom a country affords its citizens, the faster it will grow and the more prosperous its citizens will be. By that reckoning, Estonia has soared to number four from number twelve, swapping places with the United States, which now trails eleven competitors ranging from Hong Kong to Chile.

For a country that sees itself as the heavyweight champion of economic freedom, America's comedown is a wake-up call. What happened? Two things. First, the eleven countries with economies that rank higher than ours are deregulating their businesses faster than we are. Second, the United States is burdening its own economy with ever-higher government spending and barriers to trade and investment. This is a major self-inflicted wound; economic freedom is the engine of America's wealth and leadership as the world's sole superpower.

A country's degree of economic freedom reflects the ability of ordinary citizens to make economic decisions on their own. It covers all levels: finding a job, starting a business, borrowing money, using a credit card. It ranges from buying a house to having a choice in health care, from being fairly taxed to being fairly treated by courts and police officers. It also includes the right to hold your own property, free from the threat of an arbitrary government takeover. The more accessible these freedoms are, the easier it is for people to work, save, invest, and consume. A free economy surges upward, putting money in millions of pockets, boosting national wealth, power, and prestige.

One corollary is that ever-expanding government entitlements—the nanny state—reduce economic freedom. The more wealth a government controls, the less remains for individuals to use as they choose. Hence, prosperity depends largely on minimizing entitlements and maximizing the wealth available to private citizens for whatever legal purpose they choose to pursue.

The index measures freedom in ten areas of a nation's economy, including taxation and government spending, trade policies, business regulation, and protection of property rights. Each country is scored in the ten areas on a scale of 1 (freest) to 5 (repressed). The average of the ten scores is the "country score," ranking each nation according to four categories—free, mostly free, mostly unfree, or repressed.

A free country should score 1 or 2 in all ten areas of economic freedom. As an economy declines, say from free to mostly unfree, it becomes harder for people to work, do business or start a business, and make money. The country becomes increasingly poor.

Economic freedom around the world is on the march: Of the 155 countries surveyed in 2005, some 86 had more freedom overall than in 2004. The other 69 had either lost ground or remained static. Estonia, the Cinderella, ranked number four and is the shining star of once repressed communist nations now shedding their shackles. But China is the looming colossus. Though still classed as "mostly unfree" economically, China, at number 112, moved up sixteen places in just one year and is continuing on the fast track to liberalization. India too is emerging as a power player on the world economic scene. With a population of more than one billion, many of whom possess a hardworking and entrepreneurial spirit, the country clearly has the potential for great economic growth. But it must unburden itself of a protectionist trade policy, which places a heavy government strain on the economy, and relax its overregulation of business. America should recognize its common interest in a friendly and prosperous India and work closely with the Asian nation to promote these reforms.

The link between economic freedom and prosperity is clear. The latest index found that the freest countries had per-capita income averaging $29,212, more than twice the average for "mostly free" nations ($12,839) and more than four times the per-capita income of "mostly unfree" countries. Even in sub-Saharan Africa, mostly free countries had per-capita national outputs more than triple the size of those in mostly unfree countries. The cure for poverty is no mystery. It is not government-to-government foreign aid. Rather, it is economic freedom.

For decades, the United States and many of our well-meaning international friends and allies have tried to help poor countries by showering them with cash to help grow their economies. It hasn't worked. Between 1980 and 2003, we spent more than $116 billion for development projects in eighty-nine countries, half of them with per-capita incomes below $765 a year. Of those countries, only thirty-two grew by more than 1 percent, and thirty-seven were worse off than when measuring started in 1980. Over the course of that twenty-three-year time frame, sub-Saharan Africa's per-capita income fell from $573 to $514—a 10.3 percent drop.

Foreign policy experts argue that the United States really can't afford to walk away from third world countries, and especially the economic disasters that now litter Africa. We know that failed countries breed rage, war, terrorists, and danger for America and Americans. We know that military intervention is an option rife with grief. Conversely, we believe that with our cash and compassion we ought to be able to create solid opportunities for people in poor countries—ways to kick-start new businesses, provide jobs, and grow their economies. Their success would be a bargain for us, if only because it would help improve our security, while also enhancing trade and bolstering the U.S. economy.

President Bush had all this in mind when he proposed in his 2006 budget to allot $3 billion for the Millennium Challenge Account (MCA), his new foreign-aid program for poor countries unequivocally committed to three goals—economic freedom, a just government, and investment in people. The MCA's key premise, based on various economic studies, is that aid works best in countries that energetically create incentives for people to behave more productively, thus encouraging growth.

The MCA was actually launched in 2002 and is run by the Millennium Challenge Corporation (MCC), which is already sitting on $2.5 billion in tax dollars that it has not yet spent, for an encouraging reason: Rather than tell countries how to spend the money, as previous dollar disbursers did (unsuccessfully), the MCC requires each recipient to first propose a comprehensive development strategy—to be funded by the MCA—and to demonstrate how that strategy would grow the economy and reduce poverty. This grassroots approach is designed to take full advantage of local knowledge and avoid any hint of past know-it-allism, much less colonial arrogance. Thus far, the MCC has identified sixteen countries ready, willing, and able to put MCA grants to work for real economic growth. They range widely from Armenia to Bolivia to Senegal. Assuming Congress approves President Bush's new $3 billion request for the MCA, those countries and others will soon be on their way—their own way—to joining the global economy as certified players.

Globalization, which reflects economic freedom, is also a key to national prosperity. According to a World Bank study, countries that participated in the global economy in the 1990s grew their per-capita income by 5 percent a year. Countries that failed or refused to do so averaged only 1.4 percent income growth; growth in some of these countries actually declined. And contrary to the fears of some naysayers, globalization turns out to be good for the poor. Their incomes rise as their economies grow. Even the environment benefits: The World Bank study found that air quality in major industrial centers of the globalized developing countries had improved significantly.

Despite all this good news, economic freedom and political freedom don't necessarily go hand in hand. As shown by China, Vietnam, and several other nations, economic freedom can produce growth and prosperity even where political freedom is limited. Democracy or representative government is hugely desirable, but linking it to prosperity is a fallacy. Although richer countries tend to be more democratic, political freedom does not ensure prosperity. The only direct link is between prosperity and economic freedom: If a country's economy is to grow, it must have a stable monetary system, secure private property rights, an impartial legal system, low taxes, minimal governmental regulation, and low barriers to international exchange.

America is still wealthy and free, thanks to strong property rights, low inflation, and effective banking and finance laws. Even so, eleven far smaller rivals now top us in economic freedom— Hong Kong, Singapore, Luxembourg, Estonia, Ireland, New Zealand, the United Kingdom, Denmark, Iceland, Australia, and Chile. By no coincidence, foreign investors seem to be cooling on business opportunities in the United States. Foreign direct investment in the United States has reversed sharply, from a net inflow of nearly $150 billion in 2000 to an actual outflow of about $133 billion in 2004.

If the United States falls further behind in terms of economic freedom, we can expect foreign investors to quit risking capital here. If the U.S. economy weakens as foreign economies strengthen, American world leadership will decline as well.

Why is our nation losing the freedom race? We see these principal problems.

Taxes

"In this world," mused Ben Franklin, "nothing is certain except death and taxes." In modern America, taxes have the edge. The corporate tax rate is now 35 percent, higher than in 106 of the 155 countries surveyed in the 2005 *Index of Economic Freedom*. The IRS tax code fills 60,044 inscrutable pages, up 50 percent in ten years. Statistics say that Americans filling out their own tax returns spend an average 28.5 hours slogging through this verbiage to what all too often becomes a fictional finish (actually, it feels more like 28.5 months). Small wonder that almost two-thirds of American taxpayers hire professionals to wrestle with the forms. All told, the U.S. fiscal burden—taxes plus government spending—ranks America a dismal 108th out of the 155 nations surveyed in the *Index of Economic Freedom*.

Trade Barriers

Trade barriers, put up to protect domestic industries, artificially raise the prices Americans pay for SUVs, textiles, lumber, peanuts, orange juice, and a host of other products. The United States has an average weighted tariff rate of 2.6 percent, in addition to many nontariff barriers, including import quotas, antidumping provisions, countervailing duties, and licensing requirements on just about everything from anchovies to wire rods.

Antidumping laws may be even more pernicious than tariffs and import quotas. In principle, these laws entitle U.S. producers to request tariffs whenever foreign suppliers sell their products in this country at lower prices than they charge in their own countries. The law's intended check to prevent abuse is that Americans requesting tariffs must show support from 25 percent of their peer producers in the same industry. But since the recently enacted Byrd Amendment enables supporters to get a slice of the government-collected tariffs, the unintended consequence is that nearly every petition gets peer approval. Result: Industries seek ridiculous protections that wind up penalizing American taxpayers, to say nothing of alienating our trading partners and decreasing our economic freedom.

To its credit, the Bush administration is now aggressively working to expand free trade through bilateral negotiations with more than ten nations, as well as aggressive multilateral negotiations in the so-called Doha Round (named for the 2001 World Trade Organization conference in Doha, Qatar). And in 2003, President Bush lifted the misguided steel tariffs he had imposed a year earlier. But other countries are far ahead of us. Hong Kong, Singapore, and Estonia are virtually duty-free.

Business Regulations

While rival countries reduce business regulations, the United States expands them. The index weighs regulations affecting myriad fields ranging from banking to foreign investment, from capital movement to the environment and start-up businesses. In nearly every area, American companies face a heavier load of governmental regulation than their overseas rivals, draining creative energy from this country's private sector.

A prime example is the above-mentioned 2002 Sarbanes-Oxley Act, aimed at improving corporate transparency and responsibility in the wake of Enron-style abuses and scandals. The law requires chief executive officers and chief financial officers to certify in writing that they understand their companies' financial statements and to show that good internal controls are firmly in place. The law's intent is to prevent accused corporate leaders from claiming innocence by virtue of ignorance of their subordinates' machinations, a tactic previously common in white-collar criminal cases.

The law's critics deem it a disaster and even one of its co-authors, Ohio's Republican representative Mike Oxley, has admitted that the law has perhaps gone too far in regulating small and midsize firms. For example, critics cite a survey by the executive recruitment firm Korn/Ferry International, which found that the law cost Fortune 1000 companies an average $5.1 million in compliance expenses in 2004. The only real beneficiaries of the act are accounting firms; KPMG has increased its college recruiting by 40 percent, and PricewaterhouseCoopers has hired more than sixteen hundred new auditors and four hundred temps to help with the added audits the law requires. To escape the new rules, large foreign companies are delisting themselves on

U.S. stock exchanges—a blow to Wall Street and a boon to the bourses in London, Frankfurt, and Hong Kong.

The power of economic freedom in Asian countries is being super-charged by their strategic investments in research and development, especially in science and engineering. While Chinese and Indian innovators keep acquiring more and more U.S. patents for ideas they invented and now own, American researchers publish fewer and fewer articles in the world's scientific journals. Between 1991 and 2001, China's research-and-development outlays jumped 350 percent, creating, among other factors, a 535 percent leap in the country's output of Ph.D.s in science and engineering.

By contrast, those fields seem to be turning off young Americans. Despite a 14 percent rise in population, we now have 20 percent fewer graduate students in science and engineering than in 1993. The decline is worsened by a sharp fall in the number of foreigners studying in our universities. Just when terrorist worries made visiting the United States much tougher, foreign students discovered far more accessible learning opportunities in Australia, Britain, and other countries. Moreover, the rise of high-tech industries in their own countries enables graduates to find good jobs at home rather than work in the now less welcoming United States. Security is clearly a priority for Americans, but the price of lost skills and outdated research labs is prohibitive in a global economy.

THE ECONOMIC FREEDOM TRAIL

As we've shown, the United States has lately begun to switch roles on the global financial stage, losing its ranking as the champion of economic freedom and emerging as a potential has-been. The world increasingly sees America as a runaway tax-and-spender, squashing its people's financial liberty under the weight of soaring deficits and a metastasizing national debt. The world sees Washington alienating our trading partners, favoring a few corporate interests at the expense of many, fumbling with half-baked solutions, and unable to enact coherent policies.

It has come to this: Estonia, until recently an integral part of the Soviet Union, is now economically eight places higher in economic freedom than America. Enough said.

What's to be done?

The recovery of economic freedom in the United States requires four basic reforms, all pursued immediately and simultaneously:

1. Lighten the Tax Burden

At 35 percent, the U.S. corporate tax rate is at least twice as high as the rates companies pay in Ireland, Chile, Hong Kong, and Iceland. Estonia has no corporate tax at all, and even Denmark, Britain, Australia, and New Zealand have lower corporate tax rates than we do. We must strive to match our competitors.

Economists such as Steve Forbes, head of Forbes Inc., and Steve Moore, president of the Washington-based Free Enterprise Fund, have proposed intriguing flat-tax options for both corporate and individual taxpayers that we will discuss momentarily. But first, let's talk for a bit about the death tax, that peculiar bit of perversity that Congress, in bizarre fashion, has seen fit to soften over the period from 2002 through 2009, after which the tax will be abolished, but for only one year, 2010. In 2011, the death-tax rate is slated to return to 55 percent. We say end the charade and eliminate the federal estate taxes once and for all.

Death should not be a taxable event—as many other countries around the world, even formerly Marxist ones like Russia, have come to realize. Twenty-four countries, including Canada, Australia, India, Mexico, China, Russia, and even Sweden, that poster child for the welfare state, have no death tax at all. And a recent study by the American Council on Capital Formation found that only two major nations have higher death-tax rates than the United States.

In addition to the immorality of taxing death, the death tax is also bad public policy. It imposes a gigantic burden on small businesses, which can be devastated by the tax when their owners die. Unbelievably, business owners pay an estimated $12 billion each year just for insurance to prepare for the payment one day of onerous death taxes. Good, predictable tax policy is critical for robust economic activity. The death tax is neither good nor predictable. It hinders economic activity in the following ways:

- Discourages saving and investment; the death tax encourages people to spend everything they make instead of investing their money to make more money in the future.
- Weakens job creation and growth; reduced investment costs America between 170,000 and 250,000 lost jobs a year.
- Holds back the economy from reaping potential investment gains; skimping on investment deprives workers of the new tools and factories that help expand productivity.
- Gives the lie to the central promise of American life—that is, the freedom and ability to create wealth; death taxes contradict the notion that working hard, saving, and living prudently allows individuals to enjoy the fruits of their labor and pass them on to heirs.

It's almost inconceivable that a country founded on the principles of freedom and opportunity continues to tax economic virtue and productivity. In the words of Virginia senator George Allen, "No taxation without respiration."

As for the income tax rates, both corporations and individuals should be given a choice between paying their present taxes or opting for a new, streamlined, flat income tax of 17 percent. Individuals would file returns the size of a postcard, with no deductions beyond personal exemptions. Businesses would have no deductions beyond immediate amortization of capital purchases. Any revenue losses from this revolutionary change would be offset as the lower tax rate triggered a burst of growth in spending, investment, and job creation, and the growth automatically brought in new tax revenues.

All of us could save time, money, and trouble with a flat tax. Our current tax code is sixty thousand pages long and includes more than eleven hundred forms and publications. American businesses and individuals spend six-plus billion hours keeping records and filling in tax returns, and the code is so confusing that taxpayers are forced to shell out more than $200 billion each year for accountants, tax preparers, and do-it-yourself software. Even IRS employees don't understand the laws they're supposed to enforce. Several years ago, a GAO survey found that IRS employees gave incorrect tax advice half the time. Compare that quagmire of confusion with the simplicity of filing your return on a form the size of a postcard.

How exactly would the flat tax work? Like a beautiful dream: Individual taxpayers would add up income from wages, salaries, and pensions only, subtract a standard personal allowance (more for families), and multiply by 17 percent. No need to worry about how to treat dividends and interest income—those taxes would be withheld and paid at the business level—or whether all your deductions were allowable or whether the Alternative Minimum Tax applied. The flat tax would get rid of all itemized deductions like the write-off for home-mortgage interest, charitable contributions, and state and local income and property taxes. On the business side, rules governing the tax treatment of pensions and deferred compensation, depreciation, international tax provisions, and uniform capitalization rules would all be erased.

Imagine a tax system free of time-consuming paperwork and gut-wrenching aggravation. And think of the billions of dollars and hours—both on the government side and the private side—that could be redirected toward much more productive endeavors.

There's more good news. A flat tax is inherently a fairer tax than a graduated or a progressive tax because it is proportional, meaning the same rate applies for all classes of income and all entities within a class. Too often, the politically well-connected and those with the resources to engage smart tax lawyers take advantage of special credits, deductions, and tax shelters to minimize their tax liability. The result is a tax system that violates the fundamental constitutional principle of equal treatment under the law. Take, for example, Senator John Kerry's megarich wife, Teresa Heinz Kerry. In 2003, Mrs. Kerry earned $5.1 million, but only paid $750,000—an effective income tax rate of only 14.71 percent. A flat tax would ensure that every taxpayer is treated the same. The only personal exemption would be based on household family size, after which taxpayers would pay a single low rate on income above their exempted amount. What could be fairer?

Just closing the loopholes would allow us to slash marginal tax rates, simply because current tax dodgers would be paying their fair share, thereby shrinking the size of the share allocated to the rest of us. A flat tax would also eliminate the double taxation of money when it is earned and then again when it is invested or saved, a feature that would provide a big boost to our nation's long-term economic growth. A faster-growing economy would, in turn, generate more tax revenue, as economist Arthur Laffer has shown.

Even the working poor who don't owe any income taxes would benefit from a flat-tax system. The way things work now, employers withhold taxes from paychecks regardless of a person's tax status; to claim their refunds and credits, poor people have to file a return. Not surprisingly, given the convoluted incomprehensibility of virtually any document written with government ink, many of the working poor feel the need to hire tax preparers to decipher even these supposedly simplified forms. With a flat tax, people earning less than the specified amount would owe nothing and pay nothing, allowing them to hold on to the cash they now pay someone else to interpret IRS instructions.

Critics will oppose the flat tax on various grounds, the most common being a fear that eliminating all deductions would cut charitable giving and decrease home ownership. But research has shown that both charity and home ownership are linked to disposable income, and disposable incomes would increase with a flat tax. Plus, the rate of home buying rises and falls along with interest rates, which, according to a study by the Federal Reserve Bank of Kansas City, would likely decline under a flat tax.

Lawmakers know they've created a monster, they just don't know how to tame it. Instead of spending our tax dollars tinkering with a broken system, Congress should simply scrap the whole thing and start over—with a fair, flat, and transparent tax. Our economy would soar as Americans of all stripes, suddenly freed from the constrictions of the tax code, started working, saving, and investing as never before. As Steve Forbes writes, "The flat tax has already produced results around the world—from Russia to Hong Kong and elsewhere. . . . It is part of a new worldwide wave of tax simplification that has implications for America's competitive position in the world economy."

There are five broad goals that must accompany any kind of tax reform:

- Ordinary Americans must be able to comprehend the tax law.
- Tax law should be a tool for raising revenue, not attempting

to alter people's behavior in a manner some government bureaucrat believes is "enlightened."

- Tax law should not punish work, savings, or achievement.
- Tax rates should be as low as possible to encourage economic growth.
- Tax rates and exemptions must be transparent.

To be meaningful, the debate over changing our tax system should address all the potential pitfalls—like how to keep politicians from making new loopholes once the flat tax closes the old ones. But in the end, getting any major tax reform through Congress will be tough. Politicians have spent years bending the tax code to engineer social policy, fashioning credits and deductions to encourage approved behaviors and to reward campaign contributors. It will take time to undo all that mischief. Besides the immediate beneficiaries of the loopholes, who will howl long and loudly, too many people—from the accountants and tax preparers to the lobbyists who make very nice livings pleading for the special interests to the legions of IRS employees who oversee and enforce the complexities—have a vested interest in keeping things just as they are, or making them even more complex.

To get the ball rolling and put pressure on lawmakers to do what's best for the people they represent, not the special interests, we endorse an idea suggested by former Oklahoma senator Don Nickles: Send all taxpayers a flat-tax return and a regular return for one year; after filling out both, the taxpayers would file the one that benefits them the most. If a majority of the returns were flat-tax forms, the current system would be dismantled.

Does anyone doubt that the current system would be on a fast track to oblivion?

2. Deregulate

The flow of new regulations continues unabated, weighing ever more heavily on business and eroding prosperity in the process. Congress should rethink the Sarbanes-Oxley Act and remove many regulations that began with good intentions but now cripple small and midsize companies. The offenders include certain health and product safety standards, plus some food- and drug-labeling requirements.

Restrictions on foreign investment and on the free movement of capital are also needless encroachments on economic freedom. Hong Kong, Singapore, New Zealand, Luxembourg, and Ireland all have more liberal rules than we have in this area. Foreigners should be allowed to invest in those U.S. sectors that are currently off limits, including nuclear energy, maritime and air shipping, broadcasting, and communications.

3. Sweep Away Trade Barriers

Protectionist tariffs, import quotas, and antidumping laws must be cleaned from the books. Antidumping laws are especially damaging. As long as they exist, American companies will have a way to get around free trade agreements and obtain protective tariffs. Their success among our special interests has already inspired similar bad laws in other countries. If free trade is to make real headway in the world, these laws must be revoked.

4. Form a Global Free Trade Alliance

This concept, first discussed in the 2001 *Index of Economic Freedom,* would be a new approach to free trade: a voluntary alliance open to any nation that qualified and wanted to join. To be eligible, a country would have to meet four criteria. It must (1) have minimum tariffs and nontariff barriers to trade; (2) be open to capital flows and foreign investment; (3) protect private property and promote business under the rule of law, enforced by a fair, independent judicial system; and (4) not impose any undue regulatory burden on entrepreneurs or business.

At present, only twelve nations could pass all four tests, but another nineteen fail only one of them.

Having joined the alliance, any member nation would have free access to the markets of all the other members, on the one condition that it must open its markets to them as well. Once the alliance was established, joining could be accomplished rapidly, with a minimum of negotiation and without infringing on sovereignty. But the more nations that become members, the more benefits the alliance would offer—and over time, it would become a self-reinforcing mechanism for promoting free trade.

Such an alliance offers the potential for a truly global world centered on free trade, one that enhances freedom, opportunity, and prosperity for the citizens of all of its member countries.

Our cause is impeccable: Who doesn't favor the American Dream, economic freedom, and prosperity? But our opponents are indefatigable. The entrenched interests that profit from the current mess will not yield easily. It will take a long, hard, well-funded campaign to wake up the country to its growing loss of economic freedom and the danger it poses to America's wealth, power, and leadership in the world.

We must seek prosperity by encouraging the small businesses that have always been the beating heart of American enterprise. Throughout history, the vast majority of new jobs have come not from our biggest corporations but from the smallest, and that will continue to be true. Today, small businesses create seven out of ten new jobs in America and account for more than half the output of our economy.

But when the pursuit of wealth in America leads to excess, and business ethics fall by the wayside—the recent scandals offer a reminder of earlier breakdowns—the ensuing problems demand the most effective and targeted government reaction conceivable. Why did the alarm bells fail to go off before significant damage was done? Where, in the best interests of the country, should new lines be drawn to ensure success and prevent excess? The bank panic of 1907 necessitated the creation of the Federal Reserve Bank. The 1929 stock market crash produced the Securities and Exchange Commission and myriad other regulators—altogether too many, we and many like-minded thinkers believe. The debacles of Enron, WorldCom, and other recent overreachers have already triggered a flurry of prosecutions and new corporate rules in Congress, some of them, as we've shown, well-meaning but either too late or too political. It's good to remember that the self-policing efforts of company auditors, not the government, first uncovered the recent problems.

Nearly all Americans are born dreamers, with boundless ideas for new ways to do things, new products and services, and whole new ways of thinking about problems. True innovation is never predictable, and even after it pops up, its long-term consequences are often a riddle: No one knew we needed computers, and for years after they appeared, we all thought they were just for crunching numbers. Now that the whole planet is computerized, hardly any American under thirty has heard of typewriters, much less used one.

Prosperity flows from innovations that become hits, from dreamers with unlikely ideas that change the world—dreamers like the American physicist Chester Carlson, who invented electro-photography, the process of instant copying that made the Xerox Corporation a success.

Right now, it's essential for government to help make the business climate friendlier to those people. Let's oppose government subsidies, tax breaks, and other favoritism that help big corporate bureaucracies get even bigger, stifling both creative employees inside and small competitors outside. If Congress really wants to nurture the American Dream, let it help combat the dream killers behind those sad signs, LOST OUR LEASE, or THANKS FOR 30 HAPPY YEARS OF LETTING US SERVE YOU. GOOD-BYE.

Fortunately, we can count on the fundamental savvy of the American people. A healthy skepticism about Congress, for example, is one of the country's saving graces. Economists Michael F. Ferguson and H. Douglas Witte recently figured out that 90 percent of the stock market's gains occur on days when Congress is not in session, apparently because many investors lie low on the days when the lawmakers are physically on hand to foment more rules and laws, especially for business. Small wonder that the Oklahoma sage Will Rogers once said, "This country has come to feel the same when Congress is in session as we do when a baby gets hold of the hammer. It's just a question of how much damage he can do with it before we take it away from him."

If we can build on that attitude—a healthy skepticism toward the notion that Washington is the savior of the economy—we think there will be a better chance to galvanize the public, light a fire under Washington, and begin restoring America to its rightful lead place in the global quest for economic freedom.

THE BOTTOM LINE

- There is a clear link between economic freedom and prosperity. And increased prosperity means increased income for our citizens.

- America's prosperity and its global leadership position are receding under the weight of too many regulations, onerous taxation, out-of-control federal spending, and protectionist trade barriers.

- Outmoded federal programs, like farm subsidies for wealthy corporations and individuals, are diminishing America's economic strength, thus leaving us vulnerable in an increasingly efficient and competitive globalized economy.

- Overregulation not only stymies risk taking, the driving engine of prosperity, but also encourages the growth of a stifling welfare state.

- Globalization reflects economic freedom and is a key to national prosperity.

- America must preserve and strengthen its economic freedom by lightening the tax and regulation burdens, abolishing trade barriers, and forming a global alliance of countries committed to free trade.

- A Global Free Trade Alliance among like-minded peoples of the world is inherently in the best interests of the American citizen and our nation.

CHAPTER 6

★ ★ ★ ★ ★ ★ ★ ★ ★ ★

Does It Make Us Safer?

An appeaser is one who feeds a crocodile—hoping it will eat him last.
—WINSTON CHURCHILL

RONALD REAGAN BEGAN his presidency in 1981 with a clear pledge to restore America's military power and our pride of place in international affairs. Honoring that promise, Reagan and his defense secretary, Caspar Weinberger, launched a rapid military buildup. Some cabinet members balked; they urged less spending on defense and more on social programs to boost the economy. Even ex-president Richard Nixon joined the naysayers, telling Reagan: "The Pentagon should not be a sacred cow."

Reagan's response was simple: "Look, I am the President of the United States, the commander in chief. My primary responsibility is the security of the United States. . . . If we don't have security, we'll have no need for social programs."

As usual, Reagan had his priorities straight. Keeping the nation safe from harm has been every president's most fundamental responsibility since George Washington took the first oath of office. As conservatives, and as this book has consistently argued, we believe that limiting government's role in the nation's life and business is essential. But we also believe that ensuring strong national security—the protection of all citizens from foreign threats—is our government's and every government's first reason for existing at all.

Here's our security test for just about any government policy: Does it make us safer?

In proclaiming America's break with Britain in 1776, our Declaration of Independence pointed out that none of the country's core values of life, liberty, and the pursuit of happiness could be ensured without a government empowered to "levy war, conclude peace, [and] contract alliances" against its foes.

In the *Federalist Papers* urging states to adopt the Constitution, Alexander Hamilton stressed the young nation's need to be prepared for war. In his words, history proves that "the fiery and destructive passions of war reign in the human breast with much more powerful sway than the mild and beneficent sentiments of peace; and that to model our political systems upon speculations of lasting tranquility would be to calculate on the weaker springs of human character."

Hamilton argued that the government's power to wage war should be broad: "The circumstances that endanger the safety of nations are infinite. . . . It is impossible to foresee or define the extent and variety of national exigencies."

More than two hundred years later, America is threatened by all varieties of fiery and destructive passions. A short list of the biggest threats includes radical Islamic terrorism, rogue states like North Korea, and emerging global powers such as China. Let's consider each in turn.

THE NIGHTMARE OF TERRORISM

The most pressing danger we currently face is the terrorist threat posed by the militant Islamists who attacked the United States on September 11, 2001, flying fuel-laden jetliners into the World Trade Center towers, the Pentagon, and a field in Pennsylvania. They ended not only nearly three thousand lives but also the illusion that two oceans protected our American homeland from evils plaguing the rest of the world.

Our swift response in Afghanistan drove out the Taliban government sheltering Osama bin Laden and his terrorist training camps. Even more important, the U.S. invasion of Iraq toppled Saddam Hussein's despotic regime and replaced it with a nascent democracy.

The ousting of Saddam marked a crucial turning point for the Middle East. If we are to win the war on terror, the people of the Arab and Muslim world must stand tall against the radical vision of Osama bin Laden and his fellow extremists. Yet in an area where oppressive regimes and a lack of opportunity prevent so many gifted people from fulfilling their potential, we cannot expect individuals to simply reject extremism in favor of the status quo. One need only talk to any of the numerous proud men who hold engineering degrees but are stuck driving a taxi in Cairo, or to a woman in Saudi Arabia who is forbidden to walk outside unless accompanied by a male member of her family, to know that the status quo does not offer inspiration to the people of the region.

Before a coalition of the willing removed Saddam from power, the Iraqi people had just two choices: Support Saddam (either actively or passively) or face the cruel consequences of dissent. The success of the nascent Iraqi government is far from assured. But what is certain is that the Iraqi people now have reason for optimism about their future, and, most important, they have the power to build a free and prosperous society for themselves and their children. America and its partners in the coalition of the willing have taken an important step toward marginalizing extremists by providing the people of the Arab and Muslim world with an inspiring alternative vision for the future.

Beyond immediate victory for the Iraqi people, this opportunity also sends an arresting message to the citizens of other countries in the region where dissent has been silenced: If democracy can come to Iraq, it is also possible in Egypt, Iran, Saudi Arabia, Syria, and elsewhere.

Though there is much to be proud of, the work is not yet done. Taliban forces still operate along the desolate border with Pakistan, and bin Laden himself remains at large. In Iraq, the conflict has triggered an insurgency that is attracting terrorist recruits from all over the Middle East. The guerrillas are driven by the knowledge that a free and prosperous Iraq will spell the end of their ability to impose their extremist vision on the Middle East. The terrorist threat is fed by distorted interpretations of Islam, the world's second-biggest (after Christianity) religion, with more than 1.4 billion adherents in 184 countries.

Despite ancient theological disputes between the minority Sunnis and the majority Shiites, mainstream Muslims long stood for tolerance, learning, and peace. But starting in the 1980s, Muslim militants began exploiting the religion's discipline as a redemptive force in failing societies—or more perversely, as a fundamentalist bomb aimed at blowing up secular dictatorships, as in Algeria and Egypt. These militants were less often poor people than frustrated university graduates, enraged at the mess in their own dysfunctional political systems. Too weak to oust their immediate oppressors, many sought renewal as guest guerrillas of the Afghan mujahideen, who eventually forced the Soviet Union to withdraw from Afghanistan in 1989. The most prominent of those foreign guerrillas was Osama bin Laden, onetime Saudi playboy turned Islamic terrorist.

Having helped the Afghans to defeat a secular oppressor, bin Laden achieved an Islamic notoriety that allowed him to turn his then minor sect, al Qaeda, into a worldwide network based in Afghanistan—a diaspora of terrorists ejected from their own countries but now firmly linked by demonic dogma, killing techniques, and modern technology, including communicating via cell phones and the Internet. The dogma derives from a kind of hijacking of Islam by radical clerics who indoctrinate children in many Arab countries. These imams infect young believers with the notion that Islam is under attack by American and Israeli infidels, who hate Muslim culture and support wealthy oppressors everywhere. The dogma holds that heaven awaits martyrs killed defending Islam. The result is a morbid ambition that drives a seemingly endless supply of believers to seek redemption in murdering vulnerable Westerners—and anyone else at the scene, including Muslim women and children—blowing themselves to bits in the process. The paradigm is 9/11, the culminating horror of many preceding attacks but by no means as horrible as the next affliction bin Laden and his ilk will try to hurl at us.

It is profoundly depressing that so many sentient human beings see suicide bombing as an act of high moral courage and a glorious exit from their blighted lives. But this is the reality that innocent civilians around the world confront every day. This is the fact that we Americans repress at our own peril.

Terrorism isn't a viable philosophy. It's a tactic, a way for weak forces to combat far stronger opponents. But the great danger now is threefold: Terrorists have access to high-power weapons; our high-tech economy is unusually vulnerable to system-stopping attacks; and terrorist success can easily lead to an intoxication with killing large numbers of defenseless people. Given God's alleged approval for such murders, plus each killer's supposed pass to heaven, we confront both motive and opportunity for massacres of civilians on a ghastly scale.

Like guerrillas and insurgents, terrorists thrive when they have inside information allowing them to conduct surprise attacks against their enemies' weak spots. Typically, this advantage derives from the tacit support of a population hostile to its government, or sympathetic, at least, to the terrorists' aims. Thus, terrorist cells spring up where governments fail—Angola, Burundi, Liberia, and Somalia, for example—and where venal rulers prove incapable of creating an environment in which opportunity exists within the rule of law and the country's own people are safe from crime, disease, poverty, and general chaos. In such circumstances, antigovernment rebels using terrorist tactics can become popular heroes, moving about, as Mao Zedong famously put it, as easily as fish swimming in the sea. But terrorist "sleeper cells" can also flourish in Muslim communities in Western nations, where they plot and carry out their monstrous crimes. Events in Britain, Germany, Italy, Spain, and even America prove the point.

Even wealthy America cannot save all the world's failing governments from plunging into chaos and the attendant terrorist plagues. Nor should we try. But we can certainly save some, as in Afghanistan. Seeking to further define the "some," Charles Krauthammer, in his treatise entitled "Democratic Realism," proposes a single criterion for U.S. intervention: where it counts. "We will support democracy everywhere," Krauthammer says, "but we will commit blood and treasure only in places where there is a strategic necessity—meaning places central to the larger war against the existential enemy, the enemy that poses a global mortal threat to freedom." In other words, in that part of the world that sanctions Arab-Islamic totalitarianism. If America could help to establish reasonable and friendly governments in these countries, then Krauthammer is right. It would cripple Islamic radicalism in the same way the defeat of Germany and Japan crippled fascism in the 1940s and paved the way for strong, democratic institutions throughout much of Europe and Asia.

Too ambitious? There are those who think so. But in the face of a growing evil bent on destroying the United States and stopping the export of democratic ideals around the world, how can we do anything less? Should we stand aside and hope the monsters who conceived 9/11 will have a spontaneous change of heart? Besides, is it not reasonable to think that those who live in oppressive, intolerant Arab cultures might, in their hearts, welcome the chance to enjoy the freedoms heretofore denied them?

ROGUE STATES AND
POTENTIAL ROGUES

Terrorists are hardly our only enemies. The end of the cold war hasn't abolished international tensions or the need for U.S. military strength to deter aggression and keep rogue states from threatening their neighbors.

The end of the chronic threat from Libya, a country that backed international terror and abetted the 1988 bombing of Pan Am flight 103 over Scotland, only calls attention to the rogue states still fomenting their mischief. Syria, for instance, which reluctantly withdrew its forces from Lebanon not long ago but still controls the government in Beirut, is linked to the assassination of Lebanese opposition leaders and promotes Hezbollah terrorism along its border with Israel. Iran, another sponsor of terrorists, is balking at diplomatic efforts to persuade its mullahs to give up their nuclear weapons program.

Considering the astounding advances in the world since the

end of World War II—jet travel, television (now delivered world-wide via satellite in high-definition format), and the Internet, to name but a few—it's remarkable that the number of nuclear powers has barely changed. Until 1998, when India and Pakistan joined the club, only the five permanent members of the U.N. Security Council—Britain, China, France, Russia, and the United States—officially had "the bomb." Other countries wealthy enough and technically able, including Germany, Japan, South Korea, and Taiwan, don't have nuclear weapons.

One key reason for the containment is that the United States has worked hard—wielding both the carrot and the stick—to prevent others from going nuclear. For decades, our allies have known they could count on our protection in the event of an attack. In the 1970s and 1980s, though, when Taiwan and South Korea attempted to step outside the circle of protection by beginning secret nuclear weapons programs of their own, the United States exerted enormous economic and trade pressures to force them to stop.

But now the equation is changing. The most intractable problem is North Korea, the hermit kingdom in the Orwellian grip of the unfathomable Kim Jong Il, a dictator whose frightening doctrine of "army first" makes the entire nation subordinate to the military and demands that the army have "the most advanced" weapons.

The center of a cult of mandatory adoration, the "Dear Leader" ruthlessly mistreats his twenty-two million subjects, using his enormous military machine, three hundred thousand full-time police, and an entire army of secret agents to keep the North Korean people in line. Kim's political prisons and reeducation camps are reported to have killed more than a million victims. In the famine of the middle 1990s, his father, Kim Il Sung, refused food aid from abroad in the name of ultranationalist self-sufficiency.

His people were told to make noodles from bark, seaweed, and corncobs. Andrew Natsios, the current administrator of the U.S. Agency for International Development and the author of a 1999 study of the North Korean famine, estimates that two million to three million people starved to death. The average North Korean now weighs half as much as his cousin in South Korea and is nearly eight inches shorter.

In reality, North Korea is nothing more than a failed experiment. The electric power flickers on and off. Wide boulevards are well stocked with skilled traffic cops but nearly devoid of cars. The whole country depends on foreign fertilizer and food gifts to prevent mass starvation.

One of the last countries fighting on the losing side in the cold war, North Korea is a totalitarian anachronism. It is also an international pariah. But, like the Iranian mullahs, Kim Jong Il is determined to push his way into the nuclear club. Clearly convinced that nuclear weapons give his regime an international legitimacy it can't earn otherwise, the Dear Leader has been dragging out the multiparty talks aimed at halting its nuclear program. The International Atomic Energy Agency reckons that North Korea has probably assembled six nuclear weapons already, and early in 2005, satellite photos suggested that Kim might be preparing to test them. He has already test-fired medium-range rockets that could deliver nuclear warheads. Highly placed defectors from his paranoid regime say that Kim would have no hesitation about using nuclear weapons. He has reportedly warned, "If we lose, I will destroy the world."

Led by China and Japan, neighboring countries are currently trying to persuade Kim to give up his nuclear program in return for economic and diplomatic favors. But any such negotiations are almost always exercises in frustration. Kim sends his people to the bargaining table, takes offense, and stalks out; he demands concessions and bribes simply to resume talking, and then spews insults at his adversaries. When he does reach a deal, he breaks his word. Time and again over the past three decades, North Korea has signed solemn agreements in return for loans, food, or industrial investment, only to renege, abruptly and contemptuously, at the whim of its leader.

But the most important country in the talks isn't North Korea. It is China. China provides most of North Korea's fuel and food, and without Chinese support, North Korea would probably have collapsed long ago. For years now, China has let the North Koreans bluster about their nuclear ambitions—maybe because North Korea takes verbal shots at the United States that China, as a major trading partner, can't. For example, a North Korean newspaper recently wrote, "[President] Bush is the world's worst fascist dictator, a first-class warmaniac and Hitler, Junior, who is jerking his hands stained with blood of innocent people." The point is, when Pyongyang speaks, it's safe to assume it's speaking with a Chinese accent.

New Arms for a New Colossus

Rogue nations are not the only powers we must be ready to face. In what has become a well-worn cliché, the United States remains "the world's only superpower," able to dominate any opponent and enforce its global will. But in the long run, it is conceivable that another power could rise to replace the Soviet Union as our global rival—and in recent years China, the awakening giant, has shown clear signs that it aims to match its booming economic power with military might.

The most pressing danger China poses is a confrontation with Washington over Taiwan, which China regards as a renegade province to be reunited with the mainland—forcibly if necessary.

China has massed troops and missiles across the strait from Taiwan and is building an amphibious strike force that could invade the island. Washington is bound by the bipartisan 1979 Taiwan Relations Act and by moral force to defend Taiwan, but there is no guarantee that we would have help from China's neighbors in Asia, who are increasingly dependent on trade with the new colossus and fearful of offending it. Australia, for instance, has already said it would not necessarily leap to Taiwan's defense and has joined major European nations in pushing to lift the NATO embargo on selling arms to China. Despite the embargo, Beijing is pursuing a general military buildup that Defense Secretary Donald Rumsfeld has described as a threat to nations across Asia. The Chinese have been upgrading their submarine fleet, their surface-to-air missile capacity, and their high-tech communications network. The Pentagon believes China may currently be spending up to $90 billion annually on its military, or three times the amount it officially acknowledges.

"China's defense expenditures are much higher than Chinese officials have publicly admitted," Rumsfeld told an Asian security conference in June 2005. "It is estimated that China's is the third-largest military budget in the world, and now the largest in Asia. . . . Since no nation threatens China, one wonders: Why this growing investment?"

It would be both foolish and dangerous to assume that conflict is inevitable. In fact, our hope is that economic reform in China will eventually bring about peaceful political reform. But until such a day, it is foolhardy for us not to be prepared.

These three big threats facing us—terrorism, rogue states, China— are perhaps only the most obvious. The fact is that the United States can always be suddenly blindsided from some unexpected direction. We live in a world of lightning-fast change; we are stretched by far-flung commitments, and ill-served by inadequate intelligence. We would not necessarily have advance warning, for example, should Pakistani terrorists assassinate President Pervez Musharraf, seize the country's nuclear arsenal, and trigger an Indian invasion, sparking war throughout the subcontinent. We might be unprepared for a plunge in the dollar so steep that foreign investors dumped their U.S. Treasury holdings, leaving us unable to finance our deficit, much less pay our war expenses. It is not inconceivable that a runaway war in the Middle East could cripple oil production in Iran, Iraq, and Saudi Arabia, shutting down half the world's industries and triggering a global depression. Nor can we forget sudden natural catastrophes—tsunamis, fires, hurricanes, plagues, earthquakes, infections immune to antibiotics. National safety requires watchmen who spend their lives preparing for even the most implausible dangers.

From a conservative perspective, the watchmen manning the Bush White House have worked hard to make Americans safer. Not everything has gone according to plan, but it seldom does. The watchmen can scarcely be accused of napping on duty, certainly not on the terrorism front: The Afghan campaign—our initial response to the 9/11 attacks—replaced the wretched Taliban with a fledgling democracy and launched a tracking system for catching and neutralizing al Qaeda operatives worldwide. Unlike disastrous past Afghan wars waged by Britain and Russia, ours worked fast and effectively—a rare case of the right war at the right time. A genuine victory.

Our Iraqi campaign, a far more ambitious move, remains unresolved. Now the insurgents are employing suicide bombers to deter Iraqi forces from taking over the task of securing their own nation under their democratically elected government. But that doesn't change the fact that the Iraqi people have been freed from decades of tyranny, unjust war, oppression, and torture. More important, the cause of freedom has been advanced throughout the Middle East. Where the United States once shunned the risks of democracy to prop up autocratic governments in the name of stability, we have now staked out a bold alternative to the terrorists' theocratic goals. We have raised the realistic prospect of a Middle East in which freedom, opportunity, prosperity, and civil society flourish.

Saddam's fate was also an eye-opener for other tyrants, notably Libya's Muammar Qaddafi. In fact, Qaddafi forthwith decided to rejoin the community of civilized nations and give up his nuclear aspirations. The details he disclosed of Libya's program exposed an international traffic in nuclear secrets and materials stretching from Pakistan to North Korea.

President Bush has encountered criticism from those who caught a whiff of Wilsonian moralizing in his foreign policy, the kind that never did succeed in making the world safe for democracy. But to his great credit, President Bush has done his best to stress the need for patience and explain to the American people that this war will not be like any other. He worked through the United Nations to build a genuine coalition of nations to aid the cause, and he and his military advisers have tried to limit the forces used. The president has enlisted sixty nations in a Proliferation Security Initiative to detect and intercept weapons of mass destruction being shipped by air, land, and sea. Two hostile regimes have been overthrown, and for the most part, the insurgency has been reduced to suicide attacks. To be sure, the war is a long way from over, but the president was not whistling past the graveyard when he told the graduating midshipmen at Annapolis in May 2005: "Our strategy is working—we are winning the war on terror."

Assuming we're on the right track, we believe it is high time

Washington politicians got a lot more serious about the obligations and requirements that go with making us safer. Many members of Congress still find it difficult to distinguish between pork barrels and gun barrels. On August 5, 2004, for instance, President Bush signed into law a $416 billion appropriations bill for the U.S. Department of Defense. He said the measure would make sure "our armed forces have every tool they need to meet and defeat the threats of our time." In fact, the bill actually slighted the needs of our fighting men and women in Iraq and Afghanistan. After loading it up with a record $8.9 billion in amendments bankrolling pork projects around the country, Congress voted to cut funds the military needed to maintain combat readiness.

Among the appropriations to pork projects deemed more important than combat readiness were the following:

- $25,000 for Las Vegas schools to study mariachi music.

- $75,000 for Wisconsin's Paper Industry Hall of Fame.

- $100,000 for the Punxsutawney Weather Discovery Center Museum, home of the groundhog.

- $469,000 to promote wild turkey hunting as a "traditional American sport."

- $1 million for brown tree snakes, found only in Guam and non-life-threatening to humans.

- $1 million to restore Alaska's Woody Island, population zero.

- $1.7 million for the International Fertilizer Development Center.

- $3 million to renovate and expand the National Packard Museum in Warren, Ohio.

- $4.2 million to the Academic Center for Aging Aircraft in Texas and Ohio, presumably awarded for "development" since the funds were requested by the Dayton Development Corporation.

- $5.5 million to Alaska's High Frequency Active Auroral Research Program (HAARP) to heat up the ionosphere in the hope of improving military communications. (Initially designed to capture energy from the aurora borealis, HAARP has blown through more than $100 million of federal funds since 1995 for a project whose viability was cast into doubt by an Alaskan geophysics professor back in 1997.)

Meanwhile, as the war in Iraq continued and the backlog of equipment in need of repair grew larger and larger, Congress cut $100 million out of the army depot weapons-maintenance operations. More than $500 million earmarked for civilian repair technicians to help troops in the field was erased. The military's "working capital funds," which go for food and transportation requirements (helicopter parts, fuel, and the like), lost $1.5 billion. Shamefully, our troops were sent into battle without enough body armor. Unarmored military vehicles were vulnerable to sniper fire and homemade bombs.

Blindness to real-world military needs continued on a number of fronts. The Senate Armed Services Committee, for instance, slashed $1.67 billion from the defense budget on the assumption that inflation would decrease in 2005, though, in fact, there was no evidence that the economy was cooling down—quite the contrary. As the Office of Management and Budget commented,

"The practical effect of these reductions would be cuts to critical readiness accounts." Yet the cuts were never restored, and our defense capabilities were further weakened.

Even when Congress actually focuses on providing new weapon systems, it finds ways to waste funds that would be better spent truly strengthening our military. Hundreds of billions of dollars are going for weapons that assume a war between the United States and another high-tech superpower. The classic case of a dysfunctional weapon is the Crusader tank.

Big, bulky, and expensive, at $23.3 million for each one, the Crusader was a dinosaur designed to fight a land war in the Soviet Union. During the 2000 campaign, George W. Bush called the self-propelled howitzer "too heavy" and "not lethal enough." Nevertheless, the Pentagon had one heck of a time getting rid of the Crusader program. Powerful champions in Congress, the U.S. Army, and the Carlyle Group were willing to battle toe-to-toe with Secretary Donald Rumsfeld to save the forty-ton behemoth.

The army, led by then secretary Thomas White, backed the Crusader as a more powerful and accurate replacement for its aging Paladin system. The Carlyle Group's interest was mainly monetary; as the owner of United Defense, the Crusader's maker, the investor group stood to profit handsomely from the 482-unit, $11.2 billion program. Carlyle is also populated by former cabinet secretaries and retired generals, who think they know a thing or two about what's best for the country, regardless of what the president and his secretary of defense might have to say. As for the senators and representatives who kept promoting the Crusader and appropriating funds to keep it alive? Perhaps it simply proves the obvious: A fat contract that sends money back home is more important than our national defense priorities. It wouldn't have been the first time that Congress overrode the decisions of Pentagon officials. But this time, Rumsfeld prevailed, canceling the Crusader in May of 2002.

Does It Make Us Safer?

Domestic politics still seem to trump the safety of Americans. *Time* magazine found that, as of March 2004, Washington had spent more than $13 billion to help states and communities deal with terrorists, but that the "vast majority" of that money had been distributed "with no regard for the threats, vulnerabilities, and potential consequences faced by each region."

For openers, to make sure there would be resources for every district, Congress passed a law requiring that almost 40 percent of federal antiterrorism funds be divided equally among the states and territories. The remainder would be distributed according to a state's percentage of the national population. As a result, the areas most likely to make the terrorists' hit list received less money than they needed; meanwhile, many areas that were unlikely targets were flooded with cash, and they spent it in all sorts of wasteful ways.

Wyoming, for example, gets about $37.74 per capita while California and New York each get less than $5.50. Alaska had some trouble finding appropriate ways to spend all its antiterrorist funds. The state suggested buying a jet for the governor, but the Department of Homeland Security discouraged that. In the end, much of the money went for such items as emergency radio equipment, rubber boots, decontamination tents, and bullhorns.

All over the nation, in villages and hamlets far from population centers, in states that rank at the bottom of every list of possible terrorist targets, billions of taxpayer dollars are being spent on unnecessary protection—dollars that might have gone to protect those communities at the top of the list: New York City, for example. Its police commissioner, Ray Kelly, told Congress in the fall of 2003 that there had been at least six separate plots against targets in the city. He said that New York's counterterrorism needs were $900 million, but that the city had received just over $200 million in federal funds. Because of that shortfall, he added, the city had been forced to pull one thousand police officers away from their normal responsibilities to do antiterrorist work. To put it bluntly, the day-to-day safety of the citizens of New York and other target cities is now threatened because our tax dollars are going to pork rather than real priorities.

In 2003, Congress actually seemed about to correct some of the ill effects of its actions. A special $100 million grant was allotted to seven "high-threat" areas: Chicago, Houston, Los Angeles, New York, San Francisco, Seattle, and Washington, D.C. Naturally, every legislator wanted a piece of the action. Within a month, the list had mushroomed to thirty cities, but the ante had been rising too, so the top seven were still in line for a big share of the pot. Then the Department of Homeland Security added another twenty cities to the list, and it cut back the pot. New York received just 7 percent of the total.

In other words, most members of Congress felt compelled to tune out the national interest and tune in to whatever local interest they believed their constituents favored. That's democracy, and we don't blame its practitioners. We do urge our fellow citizens to examine more carefully our government's behavior—and to speak out loudly and clearly when that behavior endangers our nation. Safety is always priority number one. As Thomas Jefferson put it, "For a people who are free, and who mean to remain so, a well organized and armed militia is their best security."

THE LESSONS OF WEAKNESS

A glance at America's recent history underscores Jefferson's point. There is no doubt that our defeat in Vietnam, added to the policies that both Republican and Democratic presidents had pursued toward the Soviet Union, brought our foreign policy to its lowest point in modern history in the 1970s. And there's equally little doubt that Ronald Reagan's muscular stance reversed that decline and brought victory in the cold war.

Much of conventional wisdom may say otherwise, but we were right to take a hand in Vietnam. Revisionists say we could not possibly have won against a nationalist movement with popular support, but they are simply wrong. The North Vietnamese leaders were dangerous communists trying to take over their neighbors, and in light of our long-standing commitment to containment, we could not stand idly by while communism advanced.

Moreover, we could have won the war. It's true that Lyndon Johnson and Robert McNamara initially fought tentatively, ruling out an invasion of North Vietnam, refusing to mine the enemy's harbors, and neglecting to cut the Viet Cong supply lines. But after 1968, when commanding general William Westmoreland was replaced by Creighton Abrams, and McNamara was succeeded by Melvin Laird as Nixon's secretary of defense, the strategy was tougher and more successful. Our troops defended South Vietnamese population centers and attacked the North Vietnamese supply centers, including sanctuaries in Cambodia. When the North's Easter Offensive failed in 1972 and the South Vietnamese forces held on to all but one of the forty-four provincial capitals, the war was effectively won. Richard Nixon ordered the mining of Haiphong Harbor and expanded bombing raids on North Vietnam.

The victory was squandered because the American public and Congress had come to see Vietnam as a "quagmire." Although Nixon's "Vietnamization" program—a strategic shift in which better-trained South Vietnamese troops replaced Americans on the firing line—was stabilizing the country, antiwar sentiment was only increasing at home. Finally, the president bowed to political necessity, and in his anxiety to pull out quickly, he forced the South Vietnamese to accept a ludicrous cease-fire that allowed North Vietnamese forces to remain in the South. Then the Watergate scandal toppled Nixon and left Gerald Ford with too little political capital to keep America's pledge to respond forcefully to any violation of the peace terms. In 1975, a much weaker North Vietnamese force overran the country and chased the last Americans out of Saigon.

We didn't lose in Vietnam because we were weak militarily: Before, during, and after the war, we could have won any set-piece battle. But we used our strength irresolutely, and our enemy did not have to win in order to triumph. He had only to avoid losing until we got tired and went home.

Irresolution was the organizing principle of foreign policy during Jimmy Carter's hapless presidency, and it was capped by the Iranian hostage crisis. After agonized debate in the White House, Carter permitted the deposed and fatally ill Shah Mohammad Reza Pahlavi to enter the United States for medical treatment. The enraged mob of Iranians who retaliated by storming the U.S. Embassy in Tehran cemented the political ascendancy of Ayatollah Ruholla Khomeini, and Khomeini kept fifty-two Americans as hostages for 444 interminable days.

The media-savvy Iranians repeatedly burned the American flag and chanted insults at "The Great Satan," the United States. "America Held Hostage" became the tagline of the relentlessly televised saga. Carter dithered. As Ken Adelman noted in the *Wall Street Journal,* it wasn't until eight days after the crisis that Carter cut off U.S. purchases of Iranian oil, and it was ten days before he froze Iranian assets in the United States. It took him nearly two months to expel illegal Iranian aliens from American soil, and five months to break off diplomatic relations and ban exports and financial dealings with Iran. When Carter finally ordered the Desert One rescue mission, it ended in a grim tableau of dead U.S. soldiers and vindictive mullahs gloating over them in the desert.

Does It Make Us Safer?

A year to the day after the embassy was seized, Ronald Reagan defeated Carter's bid for reelection. The mullahs then negotiated the release of the hostages, but spitefully held on to them until Reagan was sworn in. On January 20, 1981, the new president took the oath of office on the Capitol steps and announced that the prisoners were free.

When the hostages came home, Reagan welcomed them with a vow of swift, harsh retaliation for any future episodes of terrorism. Then he set out to bolster the nation's weak-kneed diplomacy and restore its military prowess to make sure his promise could be kept. With one big stroke, he made our country far safer.

Reagan also decided to win the cold war.

This dismayed his Democratic opponents and many of the nation's allies, and, as we noted at the beginning of this chapter, disconcerted many of Reagan's own administration officials. Ever since Harry Truman's administration, U.S. policy toward the Soviet Union and its allies had been to contain them within their sphere of influence by maintaining diplomatic alliances and a military balance that relied on the recognition that nuclear war would mean annihilation for both sides—in the jargon of the times, MAD, mutually assured destruction.

To Reagan, this concept was truly mad. It was immoral and unsafe. At bottom, the goal of his policy was to eliminate all nuclear weapons and free the world forever from nuclear terror. He carefully advanced his plan to develop a ballistic missile defense—"Star Wars," his Strategic Defense Initiative (SDI)—as a technological and moral alternative to MAD, and he pushed SDI as a way to cast doubt on the effectiveness of nuclear weapons and thus help bring the Soviets to the bargaining table. The missile defense card was to prove a key to the eventual outcome of the battle between the two superpowers.

But in the years after the Cuban missile crisis, which very nearly ended in mutual destruction in 1961, Western policy in the cold war added another element to containment: the theory of détente. This was the idea that tensions between the West and the Soviet empire could be slowly defused. If commercial and cultural ties could be nurtured, they would make war less likely and promote understanding and shared values. The cold war could slowly warm into a long truce and finally true peace.

Ronald Reagan didn't buy it. To him, communism was truly the "evil empire" he branded it, and it was dangerous and immoral to talk of compromise and shared values. He thought the containment strategy was working too slowly, and that in combination with détente, it was actually working to the advantage of the Soviets. But most important, he believed that the Soviet empire was riddled with weaknesses that could be exploited to undermine the system. When the West had the upper hand, it would be time to negotiate for truly verifiable agreements.

The Soviets knew, and Reagan suspected, that the economy was their Achilles' heel. With a combination of flat-out lies and adroit disinformation, they had persuaded the world (and, critically, the CIA) that the Soviet economy was churning out $6,500 in goods and services for every Soviet subject, fully 46 percent of the U.S. output per capita of $14,000. The CIA's analysts reckoned that military spending ate up only 14 percent of the Soviet gross domestic product.

Neither Reagan nor his CIA director, William Casey, believed either of those figures. If you looked at the actual country rather than its government-manipulated statistics, Casey argued, the Soviet Union was in almost desperate shape. Except for the elite, most Russians were poorly housed, with extended families crammed into tiny apartments. By the Russians' own count, only two-thirds of Soviet homes had running water, and fewer than 2 percent of households had automobiles. Central planning had made the economy sclerotic and inefficient. The Soviets were burning three times as much energy per unit of production as the market economies of Europe; they could get only a fifth as much paper and cardboard from a given quantity of timber as the Swedes or Finns could produce. The transportation and marketing infrastructure was so poor that crops rotted in the fields while grocery shelves were empty. Despite vast reserves of coal and oil, Russians shivered with inadequate heat through their bitter winter.

In reality, Casey concluded (and actual figures later showed), the Soviet economy was only one-sixth the size of ours. In that light, Soviet military spending was soaking up one of every three dollars of output. For all their capacity for suffering and sacrifice, the Soviet people had to be nearing their limits; already the government was subsidizing food prices to stave off unrest. To Reagan, this added up to vulnerability. The Soviet empire could be defeated, not in some long run but in the decade of the 1980s. As he was to write in his autobiography, its economy was in such bad shape "that if the Western countries got together and cut off credits to it, we could bring it to its knees."

Reagan's grand strategy, backed by critical allies that included the principled British prime minister Margaret Thatcher and Pope John Paul II, was to force the Soviets into a competition they could not win, applying pressure at every possible point of leverage. The centerpiece of this strategy was to overwhelm the Soviet economy by forcing it to produce more and more weapons. In 1980, the Soviets, seeing themselves as leading in the race, pushed for a nuclear freeze and disarmament to make their advantage permanent. Reagan knew that, for our own safety, the United States had to catch up, but he decided to do it by stressing weapons that would make the Soviet arms obsolete and force Moscow to try to match them, which he judged would strain the Soviet economy to the breaking point. He raised the defense budget every year, for a total increase of 51 percent in just five years. Procurement allocations actually doubled; navy secretary John Lehman even persuaded Capitol Hill to bankroll a six-hundred-ship navy to make America supreme on the world's seas. Sophisticated new antitank weapons, antisubmarine sensors, and fighting ships were deployed.

The three-to-one Soviet edge in tanks on the battleground of Europe was still there, but it didn't matter anymore, since our new tanks could stop them. A top Soviet official said so in 1985 and was removed from his job in short order.

In this hotly competitive game, Reagan's trump card was the SDI. Both he and Weinberger were strong believers in the potential of a system that could shield America by destroying incoming nuclear missiles, and they enlisted research support for the effort from Britain, Germany, Italy, Israel, and Japan—a total effort the Soviets knew they could not match. In desperation, Moscow lashed out with some of the ugliest tactics of the cold war: Some European SDI advisers turned up dead, and a number of SDI-related facilities were bombed in Europe.

In the United States, there was widespread political skepticism that a missile defense system could be made to work. The Russians, on the other hand, were terrified that it would. Oleg Gordievsky, a KGB officer in London, gave British agents documents showing that Soviet military officials thought the SDI system might prove 90 percent effective. Reagan loved that; he showed visitors a cartoon of a couple watching a pundit scoffing at SDI, to which the wife retorts: "Well then, why don't the Russians want us to have it?" And just as Reagan had expected, the Soviets pushed up military spending yet again: If only one in ten Soviet missiles could get past SDI, they would have to build still more missiles.

Does It Make Us Safer?

By 1986, the economic strains were exposing the rifts in the Soviet empire. In Poland, Lech Walesa's labor union, Solidarity, had become a political force, and in 1988 Gorbachev conceded that its cooperation was needed to govern Poland; the union was legalized in 1989. That same year, the Berlin wall came down as the communist government of East Germany crumbled. In 1990, Chancellor Helmut Kohl presided as Germany was reunified. That same year, Walesa was elected president of Poland. As Soviet leaders had long feared, the desire for freedom was contagious: Estonia declared home rule. When Gorbachev tried to squelch the bold move, thousands protested in Georgia and Lithuania, and even greater turmoil rocked the republics of Azerbaijan and Armenia.

The last twitch of the evil empire came on January 13, 1991, when Soviet tanks killed 14 protesters and injured 230 in the streets of Vilnius, Lithuania. A week later in Moscow, nearly a hundred thousand demonstrators marched on the Soviet parliament, calling for Gorbachev's resignation. When he yielded to Boris Yeltsin, the Soviet Union was history. Without firing a shot, as Margaret Thatcher memorably put it, Ronald Reagan had won the cold war. America, and indeed the whole world, was far safer than it had been for more than fifty years.

A SAFER WORLD

As President Bush has said, we are winning the war on terror in Afghanistan and Iraq. But as we have pointed out, our country is in imminent deadly peril of a terrorist attack here at home. The specific threats suggest their own solutions. The president and John Negroponte, the director of national intelligence, must persuade the various intelligence services to work together for the common good. We must apply common sense and good technology to make commercial air travel safe and extend those precautions to general aviation. We must find ways to guard our ports and transportation infrastructure, our nuclear plants, and our chemical industry. The Homeland Security Department must help emergency responders across the country coordinate their communications and plan together for crises.

We must stop being blind to the threat posed by our porous borders and the inadequate way we now defend them. Thousands of illegal immigrants sneak across the Mexican border every night; between twelve million and twenty million are estimated to be in the United States at any given time. Any of them could be terrorists, with weapons of mass destruction in their knapsacks and suitcases. In the spring of 2005, a band of self-appointed "minutemen" showed how effective reinforcing the border patrol could be. More than eight hundred volunteers from forty-four states manned two stretches along the Arizona border, including one along a dirt road near Naco, where the only barrier between the United States and Mexico is a feeble barbed-wire fence. The volunteers spent a month standing watch round the clock, seven days a week. Whenever they spotted illegals crossing the border, they called law enforcement officers to make arrests. The results were impressive. During the corresponding month a year earlier, Border Patrol agents caught sixty-four thousand illegal immigrants along the same stretch manned by the volunteers. This year, because of the minutemen vigil, the agents caught only five thousand, meaning that at least one hole in the border was relatively plugged, reducing illegal entries by 78 percent.

It is vital to our safety to put more law enforcement officers on that beat—and to back them up with modern technology that can detect and stop intruders.

If we want to win tomorrow's wars rather than fight yesterday's wars, then technology, as Reagan taught us, will be a key factor. It has already transformed our fighting abilities. Attacking Iraq, carrier-based aircraft could hit six hundred targets a day—three times the number engaged in the Persian Gulf war just a decade earlier. A Hellfire missile can kill Iraqi insurgents hiding on one floor of a building without destroying the floors above and below the target. The president plans to spend $78 billion on transformational weapons in his second term, and an additional $275 billion for research and development of still more sophisticated weapons.

But what we really need are weapon systems and support specifically designed to combat terrorists and engage in the full range of limited conflicts we are likely to face. We need better electronic detectors, plus language training and informants able to penetrate terrorist networks. We must be quick, flexible, and creative in our strategy and tactics, and the tools we use must reflect those needs. Combining old-fashioned army techniques with the best of newfangled technology, some of our fighters in Afghanistan rode into battle on horseback and used global positioning satellites to call in air strikes on the enemy. It is just that kind of flexibility and use of advanced technology that will be needed to win wars in the twenty-first century.

Making America safer also requires tougher thinking about our weaknesses, the holes in our defenses that smart enemies look for. Consider the fact that today's U.S. military is so dominant that no other nation could possibly defeat us on the battlefield. Paradoxically, that very power makes us weaker in the sense that it forces our enemies to surprise us with unconventional weapons for which we are not prepared. Exhibit A: the 9/11 attacks using civilian jetliners to kill thousands of civilians—a terrorist attack that the American military had absolutely no chance of preventing.

Or consider the paradox of Iraq: Our invasion broke all records for military brilliance and speed, yet a vicious insurgency is still raging three years later.

Meantime, we can't afford to overlook the emergence of nuclear-tipped ballistic missiles capable of hitting the U.S. mainland. We have good reason to believe that China, North Korea, and Pakistan have either developed such weapons or soon will.

This is one danger we're striving to solve. Taking a leaf from Ronald Reagan's book, good minds are focused on stopping any nuclear missiles that a terrorist group or rogue nation might one day launch at us. Ten long-range missile interceptors were deployed in Alaska and California in the summer of 2004, designed to knock down incoming warheads while they are still in flight. The bugs are still being worked out of this system, but it holds great promise—and even an imperfect defense is better than none at all. And two more layers of missile defense are in the development stage.

In the long run, if we want to make America truly safer, we must quit allowing our security to become a mammoth gold rush for opportunists. No more politics as usual. We must get really serious: This is our freedom and these are our lives at stake. We citizens are the only people with the power to make all our representatives in Congress start behaving as if our country was in the kind of peril that actually exists. It is long past time to hold them accountable—but they will change their behavior only when they sense real concern at the grass roots. It has never been more important for the United States to have an informed, active citizenry ready to pounce when Washington goes the wrong way.

America has shown that it can act firmly against rogue states, changing their regimes and freeing their people from murderous despots. If diplomacy fails to make Kim Jong Il or the mullahs of Iran see reason, we must be prepared to invoke that last resort again. As President Bush has made clear, we have taken the offensive: "We're denying the terrorists sanctuary and making clear that America will not tolerate outlaw regimes that provide safe haven and support to terrorists. . . . We will not allow mass murderers to gain access to the tools of mass destruction."

When it comes to North Korea, the Chinese themselves may be starting to realize that a nuclear neighbor isn't in their best interests. "The appearance of nuclear weapons on the Korean Peninsula does not serve the interests of the region and any country in the world," Foreign Ministry spokesman Liu Jianchao said recently.

That's the key point. China may enjoy watching the North Koreans thumb their noses at the United States, but if Pyongyang goes nuclear, Beijing is much closer to the potential fallout. China shares a border with the North Koreans and its famously unpredictable Dear Leader, Kim Jong Il. The Chinese are right to worry that their protégé might end up using his nuclear toy against them.

One more point for Beijing to keep in mind: If North Korea goes nuclear, the region's democracies probably will too. South Korea and Japan would have little choice but to take defensive measures, especially since North Korea has already test-fired a missile over Japan. If North Korea justifies nuclear weapons programs by pointing to some American threat, what's to prevent Taiwan from claiming that Beijing's recent "antisecession law" requires a similar reaction?

Every nation has to adjust its foreign policy so that it continues to serve the specific interests of its own people. Historically, the best defense against a foe with nuclear weapons has been to build your own. Japan already has the nuclear reactors, the technology, and the money to build nuclear weapons. South Korea and Taiwan aren't far behind. No doubt, all three could turn out nuclear weapons more quickly and efficiently than North Korea could.

Imagine that you're China's leader, Hu Jintao. You're bordered by nuclear Russia and India, with Pakistan (and possibly Iran) nearby. Would you really want to add a nuclear Japan and South Korea? Worse still, would Mr. Hu want to see Taiwan adopt a North Korean strategy of survival?

So the future is up to Beijing. It can either use its influence to block North Korea or accept that the United States would let our allies protect themselves with nuclear weapons. That's a future we'd all prefer to avoid.

As Secretary of State Condoleezza Rice has acknowledged, one of our greatest tasks is to find the right balance in our policy toward China. Writing in *Foreign Affairs* in 2000, Dr. Rice pointed to the inherent contradictions in China's trying to maintain both its economic dynamism and the Communist Party's monopoly on power. Yet to become more fully integrated into the international economy, China must become a more open and transparent society that encourages the growth of private industry. As the economic problems associated with failing banks, stagnant state enterprises, and increased unemployment multiply, so too will the intensity of the struggle within China.

But, as history has shown in cases ranging from Chile to Japan, economic liberalization can be a powerful force for promoting political liberalization. Given that history, it is clearly in America's interest to support those in China and elsewhere who desire expanded economic opportunities. Meanwhile, President Bush should continue to press the Chinese leadership on the issue of human rights—even though our power to persuade remains limited by Beijing's still-rigid political grip. But opportunities abound in the Internet age, and in the more traditional conduits of educational exchange and training, to spread American values. We must seize those opportunities. In the end, information, coupled with the explosion of successful entrepreneurs within China whose success derives from capitalism, not communism, is likely to have a truly liberating effect on the Asian giant.

Yet we must not let our faith in the political power of economic freedom blind us to the fact that China is still a potential threat to stability in the Asia-Pacific region. As we said, Defense Secretary Rumsfeld has made plain that Beijing is already engaged in a general military buildup. Its exploding economic capabilities can easily be diverted to further expanding its military power. Dr. Rice has stated bluntly that "China resents the role of the United States in the Asia-Pacific region. This means that China is not a 'status quo' power but one that would like to alter Asia's balance of power in its own favor. That alone makes it a strategic competitor, not the 'strategic partner' the Clinton administration once called it. Add to this China's record of cooperation with Iran and Pakistan in the proliferation of ballistic-missile technology, and the security problem is obvious. China will do what it can to enhance its position, whether by stealing nuclear secrets or by trying to intimidate Taiwan."

Whether or not China succeeds depends in large measure on what we do to counter its negative aspirations. We must stand strong as a military power in the region, maintaining close ties with Japan and South Korea, while also paying attention to India's emerging role. Finally, we must not back away from our commitment to a free and democratic Taiwan. It's clear that our policy toward China requires a subtle balancing of competing interests and strategies to encourage a democratic transformation through economic interaction, while also maintaining relative peace in the region until such time as that transformation leads to freedom for the Chinese people. But, in any event, we must not shy away from standing up to Beijing if need be.

In the end, the battle to make America safer will be a battle for people's hearts and minds. Public diplomacy, actually reaching out to citizens of other countries directly, must become a significant part of America's international conduct. We must not only kill and capture terrorists, but also deter recruits from joining their cause. Secretary Rumsfeld has defined five broad categories of people in the war on terror: our allies, those leaning in our favor, neutrals, those leaning toward Islamic radicalism, and the hard-core terrorists. To win the war, we must kill the committed terrorists and slowly but surely shift the others in our direction. It is crucial that we convince a significant number of people in the Muslim world to be actively on our side. This is a considerable challenge: A Zogby International poll in 2003 found a favorable view of the United States among only 14 percent of Egyptians, 11 percent of Jordanians, 9 percent of Moroccans, 3 percent of Saudis, and 11 percent of citizens of the United Arab Emirates.

Just as Ronald Reagan's policies of strength were a necessary precondition for winning the cold war, President Bush's ambitious Middle East vision can open the door for a new birth of freedom. But we must spell out that vision and make it real for the people whose lives it can change. America needs a strong policy aimed at neutralizing the small percentage of Muslims who are actively helping al Qaeda and winning over those who have sat on the sidelines.

It is astonishing how little public opinion polling our government does in other nations, and how irrelevant much of what it does survey can be. But any effective effort at public diplomacy must measure what opinion actually is and how it changes, feeding back the results to shape what gets said and how. To that end, we propose the formation of an independent research organization to track foreign public opinion. Called the Corporation for Foreign Opinion Analysis (CFOA), it would hire foreign specialists to listen, conduct surveys, ask questions, and analyze foreign opinion. Purpose: to help our government sharply improve its efforts to change foreign opinion.

CFOA's reports would provide the basis for a comprehensive communications strategy. The strategy, in turn, should be approved by the president and coordinated by a senior staffer of the National Security Council. And the message we deliver should not be propaganda, but a statement of the principles we stand for and the benefits of freedom, free markets, and the rule of law. The message must be consistent, but its style and tone should be fine-tuned to appeal to our different audiences and packaged to reach different ethnic, religious, and demographic groups.

From the president down, our entire government must see this effort as a top priority and a long-term commitment. Foreign public opinion is at least as important to U.S. national security as American public opinion is to an election.

The State Department funds a magazine called *Hi,* for instance, published in Arabic and English, with the aim of "building bridges of understanding among our cultures." The aim went wildly awry in an article called "Sharp Dressed Men" that began, arrestingly: "Real men moisturize." The article described a public relations executive not only moisturizing (with separate creams for the face and body) but getting facials, manicures, and pedicures. "He's a refined, evolved, sensitive guy," the article confided. "In a word, he's a metrosexual." The effect of this can only be imagined in a culture of exaggerated masculinity where thieves are flogged, "honor killings" for lost virginity are common, and nudity is seen as shameful. And this is produced with our tax dollars.

In the long run, the battle to make America safer is part of a larger cause—the battle to make the free world safer and, indeed, to make the whole world freer. Victory will come only if representative government prevails, because freedom is the one force strong enough to stop tyranny and terror. But as President Bush said in May 2005, "Liberty is on the march. In the last eighteen months, we have witnessed a Rose Revolution in Georgia, an Orange Revolution in the Ukraine, a Purple Revolution in Iraq, a Tulip Revolution in Kyrgyzstan, and a Cedar Revolution in Lebanon—and these are only the beginning." Spreading democracy and bringing freedom to millions of people who have never known it is a noble cause; but it also pays a practical dividend: It is the best way to make America safer.

THE BOTTOM LINE

- We must make sure that strong national security is the administration's and Congress's primary concern; funds must not be squandered on pork-barrel politics.
- We must fight terrorism at home and abroad, with force when necessary and with unceasing efforts to spread democracy around the world.
- We must contain rogue nations, using diplomacy when possible but recognizing that our military strength might have to be called into play to deter aggression and keep rogue states from threatening us and their neighbors.
- We must not let down our guard with China, recognizing that it may be the world's next superpower. Assuming that

conflict is inevitable would be both foolish and dangerous, but being unprepared would be even more foolhardy.

- Public diplomacy must be restored to its critical role in winning the hearts and minds of people around the world. The more people understand America's message of freedom, opportunity, prosperity, and a civil society, the safer we all will be.

CHAPTER 7

★ ★ ★ ★ ★ ★ ★ ★ ★ ★

Does It Unify Us?

A house divided against itself cannot stand.

—ABRAHAM LINCOLN

FROM THE NATION'S BEGINNINGS, our leaders have warned that strength can be found only in unity. George Washington said that "the bosom of America" was open to all, but only if they were willing to be "assimilated to our customs, measures, and laws: in a word, soon become our people." Alexander Hamilton said the nation's future would depend on its citizens' love of country, lack of foreign bias, "the energy of a common national sentiment, [and] a uniformity of principles and habits." The one sure way to bring down America, said Theodore Roosevelt, "would be to permit it to become a tangle of squabbling nationalities," each insisting on its own identity. And Woodrow Wilson said flatly, "You cannot become thorough Americans if you think of yourselves in groups. America does not consist of groups. A man who thinks of himself as belonging to a particular national group has not yet become an American."

And, in fact, America's classic immigrants did see themselves as individuals, ready to forsake their old allegiances and take on a new national identity. As John Quincy Adams told a visitor, "They must cast off the European skin, never to resume it. They must look forward to their posterity rather than backward to their ancestors." America has always sought to help immigrants incorporate their unique values and culture into the melting pot that is America. Becoming American has nothing to do with birth, ancestry, or ethnic identity; it is a state of mind, heart, and beliefs.

In the past, new citizens of this great country were welcomed with a solemn ceremony befitting the commitment they were making. They had been through a rigorous testing process, demonstrating their command of English in a probing interview with an examiner of the Immigration and Naturalization Service (INS); they had proved their moral character and answered questions covering the history, culture, and political heritage of their adopted country. Then, in a formal courtroom, a black-robed federal judge would lead them through the oath of citizenship, telling them what it meant to be citizens and how to live up to their new responsibilities. "Today you are Americans," he would tell them, and he might well add, "You may call yourself 'an American of Guatemalan descent,' but first, last, and always, you are an American."

Today's new citizens have no such uplifting experience. They have passed a standardized, multiple-choice test, often administered in their native language rather than in English, that resembles a trivia quiz ("Who was the first president? How many states are in the U.S.?"). They have demonstrated their English in an equally perfunctory chat with an interviewer who knows they have passed the test; if they can write down a semblance of just one of two dictated sentences ("The American flag is red, white, and blue"), they pass—and spelling and punctuation don't count.

Then, still in the nondescript local office of the INS, a bureaucrat reads them the oath. If they have brought their two standard photos, they can go straight to the passport office to be set up for their next trip "home"—to China, Honduras, Poland, or Sierra Leone.

This scene is sadly symbolic of the way Americans of all stripes are being taught nowadays to think about their citizenship and their national identity. The national motto, *E pluribus unum,* remains on the books: Out of many, one. But the unity that we once prized is eroding. What used to be seen as a melting pot, producing distinctive Americans from a hodgepodge of nationalities, has cooled to a salad bowl whose contents retain their original shapes and flavors.

It is a dangerous trend, and the consequences of losing our national identity are made horrifyingly evident by savage acts of terrorism in Spain, the Netherlands, Britain, Pakistan, and elsewhere. European-born sons of Muslim immigrants, seemingly ordinary middle-class children raised amid the freedoms bestowed by democratic institutions and educated in the best Western schools, have calmly blown up Spanish and British commuter trains and buses, beheaded *Wall Street Journal* reporter Daniel Pearl, and murdered Dutch filmmaker Theo van Gogh in grisly fashion, in broad daylight. There is no remorse, no shame; gripped by fanatical zeal and apparently obsessed by their hatred of democracy, these assassins rejoice in their barbarism.

What has gone wrong? How have these evil individuals managed to slip so easily into our midst without our noticing? Britain may be the current poster child for the failure of Western Europeans to successfully assimilate their immigrants, but few, if any, of its neighbors have done much better. And the story is not necessarily better in the United States, where the 9/11 hijackers lived undetected until they committed their heinous acts of war.

Practicing what Giles Kepel, of the Institute for Political Studies in Paris, calls "a kind of politically correct apartheid," immigrants to Western Europe, mainly Muslims, were encouraged to remain aloof from the broader society. Host countries were blissfully ignorant of problems within their immigrant enclaves until the spate of terrorist incidents changed perceptions and heightened fear and disapproval of Muslims, which further hinders assimilation.

France, for instance, has huge slums populated with immigrants alienated from French culture. Having successfully absorbed earlier waves of European immigrants without losing its French identity, France now struggles amid the deluge of third world arrivals. One visible sign of that struggle is its ban on Muslim girls' wearing their traditional head scarves in public schools. France wishes to preserve its republican tradition of religion as a private affair, but Muslims, probably unaware of France's centuries-old battle between clerical and anticlerical forces, perceive the prohibition as discrimination solely against them. As a debate rages over whether outside cultures can be safely incorporated, or whether they must be staunchly resisted, France, in its own inimitable fashion, is drawing plans for a new Museum of Immigration. No one is quite sure of the museum's purpose, but whatever it is, its effect on the likes of Idris Bazis will probably be minimal.

Parisian-born Bazis, the son of Algerian immigrants, abandoned his work as a building surveyor to become a soldier of Islam. In February 2005, the man born and raised in a city that prides itself on its civilized, secular culture blew himself up in a suicide bombing in Iraq. Of the five million Muslims who call France home, most abhor the path of violence, yet a number of French-born Muslims have made disturbing headlines. Zacarias Moussaoui, part of the 9/11 conspiracy, is a Frenchman, for example, as are two accomplices of the shoe bomber Richard Reid, who tried to blow up a Miami-bound flight from Paris. Accounts have emerged of Frenchmen plotting to bomb embassies and crowded markets, gaining military training via underground networks, fighting and dying in Iraq, and overseeing cells of homegrown militants.

Having long ignored immigrant populations, failing to give them compelling reasons to think of themselves as British, or French, or Dutch, or even European, Western Europe and the world are now reaping the unholy harvest of this neglect.

The United States has a different history than Europe, of course. As a nation of immigrants, America was founded on a set of exalted ideas of equality and God-given rights, and it endured a bloody civil war in service to those principles. But when our national unity is watered down, so is our resolution and our readiness to respond as a nation to the challenges we face.

Let's be clear: We aren't preaching that all Americans must march in lockstep. Unity does not mean uniformity. A bland sameness in thought, word, or deed is the antithesis of the American perspective. The continuing strength and vitality of our country comes in large part from our differences and disagreements, from the unimpeded flow of ideas and experiences, from the incredibly varied mixture of cultures and traditions that we cherish—all of which works to broaden our collective intellect. Like an alloy, we are harder and tougher because our base metals are mixed.

Our unity, however, springs from our basic national identity and values: Whatever our ancestry, accent, or political preference, we are first, last, and always Americans. We consent to be governed. We prize freedom, independence, decency, and opportunity. We are idealistic; we aim to be the shining city on a hill. And we know that we all depend on one another. As Ben Franklin famously told the signers of the Declaration of Independence, "We must all hang together, or assuredly we shall all hang separately."

Today, none of that can be taken for granted. America actually encourages its ethnic groups to cherish their differences and remain loyal to "the old country." Dual citizenship, once forbidden, is now routine. Even when immigrants mean to stay and become citizens, our system now demands so little of them—in the way of learning our history, mastering our common language, and demonstrating loyalty and commitment—that citizenship is devalued, if not trivialized. Our system even defers to the newcomer's former identity. Criminal defendants have argued, with at least some success, that their crimes are justified by their native culture. In 1989, a Chinese immigrant to New York, Dong Lu Chen, murdered his wife with a hammer because he suspected her of infidelity. After an anthropologist testified that female infidelity is anathema in China, Dong got off with five years' probation. It would be a terrible harbinger for the future if this wife-murderer was let off the hook because our society had lost confidence in its values.

Above all, national unity presupposes loyalty—that all of us identify with America and support its causes. But the system no longer demands even that. In Los Angeles in February 1998, a Gold Cup soccer game between Mexico and the United States brought out a fervent crowd of 91,255 fans, most of them Mexican immigrants. They waved Mexican flags, booed when "The Star-Spangled Banner" was played, and pelted the American team "with debris and cups of what might have been water, beer, or worse." When a few fans tried to raise an American flag, they were attacked with fruit and cups of beer. "Playing in Los Angeles is not a home game for the United States," observed a *Los Angeles Times* reporter.

Reasonable readers may doubt that any of this is much different from what happened in previous waves of immigration in the United States. After all, in the great influx of the early twentieth century, there were vast clusters of Italian, Chinese, and Jewish immigrants in which only the children learned more English than they needed to navigate the nearby streets. By one count, fully one-third of those newcomers found America such a bad fit that they returned to their original countries.

In those days, however, all the institutions of American society were focused on assimilating immigrants. Schools, churches, and social workers all instilled patriotic values and the benefits of becoming American. Gaining citizenship was an ordeal, involving hours of classes and fearsome confrontations with authority. And the prize was cherished: A new citizen was hailed at work and celebrated in the neighborhood as a person who had been proven worthy of citizenship in the United States and would never have to look back. In fact, they seldom did. It is fashionable now to deplore the classic immigrants' disdain for their roots and the fact that second-generation ethnic Americans had little use for their parents' native language and culture. But this attitude was surely one of the keys to assimilation and national unity.

E PLURIBUS . . . PLURIBUS

There can be no doubt that many of America's institutions no longer promote assimilation, and the result disturbs thoughtful observers across the political spectrum. The distinguished liberal historian Arthur M. Schlesinger Jr. wrote a book, *The Disuniting of America,* arguing that the new stress on ethnicity has benefits, but that "its underlying philosophy is that the United States is not a nation of individuals at all but a nation of groups, that ethnicity is the defining experience for Americans." This dogma, he warned, "replaces assimilation by fragmentation, integration by separatism. It belittles *unum* and glorifies *pluribus.*" The noted conservative

William E. Simon Jr. has sounded the same alarm: "There are disturbing signs that here in America difference and separateness are becoming more pronounced than unity and harmony." And the distinguished cultural historian Samuel P. Huntington's new book, *Who Are We?*, warns that citizenship has been devalued and that a revival of national identity is crucial to America's very survival.

What has gone wrong? We believe Simon is right in tracing the trend not to any basic change in the immigrant population—today's newcomers are as willing as ever to be assimilated—but to the cultural revolution of the 1960s, which was led by elite young students and the postcollege generation of the day. In the backlash to the war in Vietnam, authority was called into question and the nation's superiority was no longer accepted. Patriotism itself became suspect, derisively equated with Rudyard Kipling's jingoism: "To be born an Englishman means winning the first prize in God's lottery." The American flag became a right-wing symbol, brandished by the people who beat up peace marchers. "Americanization" was seen as coercive, even ruthless—in the catchphrase of the day, the equivalent of destroying a village in order to save it.

The cultural relativists largely succeeded in imposing their attitude on the political scene, and, as usual, the pendulum swung too far. If nothing was better than anything else, nothing could be much worse, either. Morals were as relative as values; the criminal, molded by genes and environment, wasn't really responsible for his or her crimes. And love of country was simply naïve and embarrassing. No less a liberal icon than Ralph Nader was brusquely rebuffed when he suggested that one hundred of America's biggest businesses should honor their country by reciting the Pledge of Allegiance at their annual meetings. Only one company agreed. Half never responded. The CEO of Aetna Insurance actually told Nader that his idea was "contrary to the principles on which our democracy was founded."

In fact, the Pledge was on the wane even in the nation's classrooms, where for decades it had marked the beginning of each school day. By one count, fewer than half of America's teachers and students now recite it.

The fading of the Pledge is both a tragedy in itself and the symbol of a greater loss to our nation. Like the flag itself, the Pledge is only a symbol of the great concepts we hold in common: individual freedom, the rule of law, opportunity, equality, and responsibility. But however routinized the solemn recitation or even a mumbling of the Pledge may become, it does serve to remind children daily of who we are and what we stand for. Its loss is one more diminution of the unity and sense of community that bind us together as Americans.

HISTORY LESSONS

If America is to unite again around our common values, we must teach all Americans—and especially new Americans and our younger generation—what that means. But education is a job now handled by governments—local, state, and national—and the first great failure of government in achieving national unity is its failure in education, beginning with the teaching of immigrants.

In many areas of our country, teaching American history has become taboo. One need only visit Abraham Lincoln's home state of Illinois to discover the truth of this sad fact. In the Illinois "learning standards for United States history," there are no measurable criteria for making sure students are learning American history. Teachers in Chicago, however, receive some guidance from the public school system—about how to teach Mexican history. They are given a 163-page guide that aims to "provide teachers with background knowledge so that the lessons will not be taught in isolation."

Learning about other peoples and cultures should be a part of any complete education, of course. But the Chicago model—where students spend two days making piñatas—goes too far; it places such a heavy emphasis on difference that it discourages national unity. The people of Chicago have the right to choose how they want to educate their children, and we would never claim to possess the authority to dictate what other people's children should be learning. We would submit, however, that most parents in Chicago agree that teaching our shared national values is more important than teaching the values of some other country. Quite simply, vocal interest groups have hijacked our nation's curricula and turned it into a mishmash of politically correct identity politics. It is time for Americans nationwide to pay attention and reclaim our children's education from those who seek to divide our country by focusing on differences rather than uniting us.

America's newcomers have been among its most precious assets over the years; we have had a genius for turning immigrants into Americans. In recent years, huge waves of illegal immigration—especially across our southern border—have come to seem far too much of a good thing; critics have complained that there are too many to digest successfully. In truth, the sheer number of illegal residents is indeed a problem and a dilemma for America, and measures must be found to slow the influx and persuade many now here to return to their homelands. But also in truth, the percentage of foreign-born people living in the United States today is significantly below what it was in 1890 and 1910, and the culture of our incoming Asians and Latin Americans is no more alien than that of the Eastern European Jews, Italians, Czechs, and Chinese who arrived and assimilated in those years. We had better focus on how they are educated when they are here. Otherwise, we run the risk of European-like immigration catastrophes.

Does It Unify Us?

The greatest mistake we have made in recent years was the vogue for bilingual education, which arose as a natural consequence of cultural relativism and the cult of diversity. Some educators argued that it was far too difficult for children who didn't speak English to learn in classes taught in the new language. Far better, they said, to conduct classes in math, history, and the sciences in the children's native language, reserving English for teaching English alone. Beginning in the Southwest and spreading to the East Coast, bilingual education began in the 1980s and reached an estimated 3,768,653 children at the start of the twenty-first century.

The results have proved the experiment a disaster. In California, Hispanic children have been shown to be delayed by a full generation in assimilating to their new country. By contrast, children in "English immersion" classes, taught only in English, have more than twice the rate of English proficiency.

Fortunately, the end seems near for this calamitous experiment. Many educators still proclaim its virtues, but faced with the figures, voters have abolished bilingual education by referendum in California, Arizona, and Massachusetts.

We have touched upon the second great failure of government in preserving our national unity: the long, slow degradation of the process of naturalizing new citizens. And the loss of ceremony and dignity in the official swearing-in that we have already described is only a symbol of the deep loss of substance and content in recent years in the education of immigrants to the United States.

It was just a year after the Constitution was ratified that Congress passed the first law dealing with citizenship and naturalization, giving the judiciary the power to create new citizens. Well into the twentieth century, the process remained much the same: Immigrants had to make a formal application to the government and then pass a test, face-to-face with a trained examiner, to prove a threshold knowledge of American civics and a working mastery of the English language. The petitioners had to have lived at least five years in the United States, be of good moral character, have an "attachment to the Constitution," and give a formal declaration of their intention to make America their home. They also had to provide witnesses to attest to their character and intent.

Over the years, the INS became known as a tough but fair agency. Some of its examiners were friendlier and more lenient than others, but, on balance, they reflected the national policy: They were the nation's judges of who deserved to be citizens, and they welcomed any good person who sincerely wanted to become an American and made the effort needed to qualify. Over the years, the rules changed and reforms were made to fit new conditions, but that basic role remained.

It wasn't until the 1980s that the system began to be overwhelmed. The problem was illegal immigration. There had always been people who sneaked into the country or overstayed tourist or student visas; despite their illegal status, many of them succeeded in winning citizenship if they proved to be hardworking and a good fit for their communities. But twenty-five years ago, a combination of factors—hard times in Mexico, a boom in the United States, and a craving for cheap labor on the part of Southwestern employers—created the vacuum that has pulled Latin American migrants across our porous southern border ever since.

The border patrols were overwhelmed, and for years Congress failed to give them the money and tools needed to stem the tide of illegal workers. This failure reflected political reality: Liberals tended to sympathize with the migrants, while conservatives were split between their law-and-order wing and the probusiness faction that sided with the Southwestern companies that could now get willing workers at wages Americans would scorn.

Finally, the Immigration Reform and Control Act of 1986

tried to tackle the whole range of accumulated problems. First, it created an effective amnesty for fully three million illegal U.S. residents, offering rapid legalization with a much lower threshold of tests. At the same time, the new law created sanctions against employers who knowingly hire illegal aliens.

Ironically, the amnesty for illegal migrants created another stampede: Law-abiding immigrants who had made every effort to comply with INS rules now resorted to fake documents and false testimony to prove they had been illegal all along, and thus qualified for the quick-and-easy process.

Immigrants had complained for years that the INS examiners had uneven standards, with some asking more difficult questions than others and insisting on higher levels of English proficiency. To meet that criticism and speed handling of the rising tide of applications, the INS revised its standard textbook for immigrants, from which the examiners had drawn their questions. Now there were three levels of texts, the highest aimed at fourth- to sixth-grade reading standards. A simplified written test of "One Hundred Questions" was developed for the amnesty class. It wasn't supposed to be used for nonamnesty applicants, but it often was—and there are indications that the "One Hundred Questions" are still being asked in some INS interviews.

In fact, the reform act signaled a sea change in the culture of the INS. From seeing themselves as guardians at the nation's gates, examiners began thinking of their role as helping immigrants over the hurdles. They sympathized with their clients' hopes and fears, knowing that many of them had a well-grounded fear of officials of any nationality. And that perception helped lead to the next and most serious softening of the standards.

In 1990, the INS brought in the Educational Testing Service (ETS), the Princeton, New Jersey–based nonprofit company that had developed the college-level Scholastic Aptitude Test, among many others. ETS was to devise a standardized test for new citizens. Even more than the INS officials, ETS decided, as one of its supervisors put it, that "we're here to help the immigrant community." To help develop the test, the service recruited a board of advisers representing the community, including Hispanic groups and the U.S. Catholic Conference. Together, they developed standards—a 60 percent grade would be passing, including writing one of two sentences from dictation—and negotiated the rules and the list of questions with the INS.

ETS says the questions were so carefully devised and thoroughly tested that the cost of development came to $5,000 per question. The results, however, are curiously bland and predictable. Among the questions: "Who was the first president of the United States? What is the supreme law of the land? Where is the nation's capital? Who is your congressman? How many states in the U.S.?" The test is now given separately from the interview; the interviewer, knowing that the applicant has passed the test, has only fifteen minutes to probe language skills, character, and background and seldom turns anyone down.

The law also permitted ETS to remove the testing itself from INS premises that might intimidate applicants. ETS did so by recruiting community organizations, church groups, and even commercial training and testing companies to administer the test. These groups are trusted to verify identities, proctor the testing, grade the tests, and report the results to the INS. Since they have every incentive to go easy on the applicants, the result is incredibly high rates of success—80 percent on average, with one commercial outfit passing 96 percent of all candidates.

Ads for the groups administering the test boast that it's "Easier than ever!" Yet the test givers pressure ETS to make it even more user-friendly, "dumbing down" the test still more. With INS approval, these groups can give the test as often as it takes an applicant to pass, and the repeat tests are variations on the original. No note of repeated failures is sent to the agency. Critics say, with some justice, that an applicant would have to be an idiot to be rejected.

At that, the applicant might get in. Even the sympathetic INS officials complain that special-interest groups are "gnawing at the rules," trying to get the requirements lowered. Applicants over fifty-five years old are already allowed to take the test in their native languages, including Spanish, Chinese, Korean, and Taga-log. References to "our country" have been stripped from the texts on the grounds that migrants might be confused about which country was meant. The INS is mulling a way to give the English test by telephone. Some groups are pushing to exempt more people from tests of English and history. And sure enough, at least one group is lobbying to exempt aged and mentally handicapped applicants from all tests of knowledge.

In some such groups, abuses of the rules are routine. The tests are often given in foreign languages to applicants too young to be exempted from English, for instance, and investigative reporters have found repeated cases of answers being passed out along with the questions. But then, the INS itself is happy to perform the same service. In 1995, a staffer for Texas congressman Lamar Smith, then chairman of an immigration subcommittee, was asked by a cafeteria worker if she could get him a copy of the test. When she called the INS, she was surprised to learn that it did give out copies before the test was administered—and even more surprised when a copy arrived with the answers enclosed.

Clearly, the bar for citizenship has been lowered to the point that only the lamest of applicants could fail to step over it. And once in, the new citizens have nothing more to prove. In former days, they had to renounce their native country; now, they may keep dual citizenship. They no longer lose their citizenship for voting in another country or serving in someone else's armed forces. In most cases, they are not even thrown out if their application turns out to be fraudulent. And while the requirement for "fitness on moral and loyalty grounds" is still on the books, it is virtually meaningless in the new age of moral relativism.

Inevitably, this lowering of standards devalues citizenship for those who get it. What can it be worth if it is so easy to achieve, if America cares so little about who is allowed in? What can citizenship mean—apart from a ticket to welfare, Medicaid, and Social Security—to people who have been taught nothing of the values and political concepts that have formed America? How can people who don't know the language understand the debate that underpins democracy? Their vote is as good as yours. Do you want them deciding America's future?

But then, Congress has also arranged it so a person can vote without being a citizen. Under the "motor-voter" act—the National Voter Registration Act of 1993—people can register to vote by requesting a mail-in form at any of several local offices, including welfare and driver's licensing agencies. Under the law, agency workers are forbidden to ask for any proof of citizenship, or to deny applicants even if they see evidence of noncitizenship. In one Texas border county, voter registration ballooned by more than 10 percent in five months when the new mandate went into effect.

Ironically, the supposed intent of the law was to protect the integrity of the electoral process and maintain "accurate and clean" registration rolls; neither goal has been advanced. Quite the contrary: The restrictions against asking for proof of citizenship have made it harder to verify the identity of voters trying to register, and the drawn-out process for confirming that someone has moved from his or her voting district has made it tougher to get ineligible voters off the rolls. It is no surprise that, in some counties, the voting-age population is smaller than the voting-roll numbers. The suspicion of fraud runs high across the country and has been documented in St. Louis, assorted Florida counties, and Georgia. The very possibility of voter fraud harms the nation by calling into question the integrity of the electoral process. It is clear that the National Voter Registration Act is deeply flawed and must be revoked.

Unity and a sense of national identity can be restored in America, but only if we all recognize the need and make the necessary effort to reform the immigration and naturalization system. We must be guided by three firm principles:

- Especially in a time of terrorism, the need to secure our borders is a top priority.

- Citizenship is not a right. It is a precious privilege that must be earned, and it is America's prerogative to choose those immigrants who are qualified to become American citizens.

- Those who join us must do so wholeheartedly. They must become Americans, understand our nation's history, and speak our shared English language.

Within these principles, much can be done. First, we must make sure that our new citizens are carefully selected and educated to become true Americans.

We must restore the mission, discipline, and attitude that characterized INS examiners for so many decades: They must become again the guardians of citizenship, the judges who bestow the most valuable prize America has in its power to give. Applicants for citizenship are not clients to be served, but petitioners whose merits must be weighed. The standards for joining us must be raised.

This doesn't imply that our immigration officials must be

Olympian or adversarial; instead, they should be fair and rigorous but impartial. They can and should have a welcoming attitude, helping immigrants learn American values and understand the American identity they are expected to take on; but they must also be strict in maintaining standards. We should develop sophisticated new learning materials, and our immigration textbooks must be deepened and strengthened to teach the real meaning of being American.

We must instill in our new citizens not just trivial factoids, but the great concepts that govern our nation: liberty, equality, the sense of fairness, the opportunity to risk and prosper or fail, and the rule of law. We must teach them the full rights and duties of citizens, not just the ritual of voting and the benefits of a passport. The requirement of a good moral character must be restored to the naturalization process, and witnesses should testify to it. We must make sure the applicants know our language well enough to participate in the great democratic debate that keeps us free, and to that end, we must stop giving tests or texts in any language but English. Finally, we must test applicants fairly but strictly to make sure they have learned enough to be Americans.

When our new citizens have won the prize, we must bestow it with dignity and honor in a ceremony worthy of the occasion. They should be sworn in with a solemn oath. The law now describes the content of that oath, but it has never been codified; words should be found to make the oath a ringing affirmation of dedication to America, renouncing any prior allegiance. The ceremony should be, as it has been for generations of immigrants, a day of pride and achievement that they will remember all their lives. And it should be a ceremony that reminds the rest of us what it means to be an American.

In recent decades, many Americans have come to regard immigration as a chronic problem, even a threat—a tide of foreigners aiming to steal our jobs, overwhelm our charities and welfare system, and undermine the American Dream. But if we can just reform the way we treat immigration and immigrants, we can make the best of them not just citizens, but Americans. Immigrants will be again what they have been throughout our history: America's greatest asset, the new blood that enriches our veins and strengthens our unity.

THE BOTTOM LINE

- America's rich diversity of peoples is at the heart of her strength and vitality, but our basic national identity and values bind us together as loyal Americans who are supportive of her causes.
- The unity that we once prized and that we encouraged our immigrants to embrace is eroding in a dangerous trend toward cultural relativism and the cult of diversity that threaten our very survival.
- Citizenship has been devalued, the standards watered down, and the naturalization process itself turned into a meaningless exercise.
- We must restore citizenship to its rightful place as a precious privilege to be earned, and raise the standards and strengthen the educational process to ensure that only qualified immigrants become American citizens.
- Bilingual education has been a huge mistake that discourages immigrants from becoming true Americans and relegates them to second-class status; we must make sure that immi-

grants know our language well enough to participate in the great democratic debate that keeps us free.

- All the institutions of American society must again be focused on assimilating immigrants, teaching them—as well as our younger generations—what it means to be an American.

EPILOGUE

★ ★ ★ ★ ★ ★ ★ ★ ★ ★

The Courage to Act

The American, by nature, is optimistic. He is experimental, an inventor and
a builder who builds best when called upon to build greatly.
—JOHN F. KENNEDY

THE FOUNDING FATHERS did not envision a country of
selfish materialists ruled by their own appetites. The Founders
fought to protect freedom for others as well as themselves. They
wanted a society that maximized liberty while minimizing
license—a moral order inviting people to aspire to do their best,
not their worst. To encourage personal virtue and ensure limited
government, the Founders placed ethical standards at the very
core of the American experiment—standards by which today's
laws, policies, and programs must be measured.

Once convinced that revolution was necessary, the Founders
knew that moral strength had to make up for their military weak-
ness. They were, after all, little more than a ragtag miscellany of
colonial farmers defying the world's then biggest superpower.
But they believed so deeply in their cause that they were willing
to put their lives and sacred honor on the line to defend it. To
overcome Britain's vast fleets and hired mercenaries, the Americans

appealed to higher law—to justice, reason, a merciful God, and the highest human values, notably individual freedom moderated by decency, dignity, responsibility, and virtue.

That precedent, we believe, is America's greatest legacy—and unfortunately now among our least appreciated. It is hard to think of any national priority more urgent than the need to reactivate the Founders' higher-law legacy.

Imagine the joy in Boston (and disdain in London) when Thomas Jefferson's incandescent manifesto proclaimed Britain's thirteen American colonies a "separate and equal" nation. No wonder his words acquired an almost biblical aura, ringing down the centuries as a unique formulation of legitimate political authority and the proper ends of government. Jefferson's purpose, he later wrote, was simply "to place before mankind the common sense of the subject, in terms so plain and firm as to command their assent." Modesty aside, he proved that a moving summons to simple justice could ignite a cause so powerful that ultimately it could not be defeated, even by all the king's men.

To a Europe chafing under increasingly shaky monarchies, the Declaration's vivid second sentence must have had the sound of crashing glass. "We hold these truths to be self-evident, that all men are created equal, that they are endowed by their Creator with certain unalienable Rights, that among these are Life, Liberty, and the pursuit of Happiness." Because these God-given rights belong equally to all persons and cannot be taken away, Jefferson wrote, governments derive their just powers from one paramount source—the consent of the governed. The purpose of government is to secure these fundamental rights. As long as governments do so, they deserve popular support. But should they betray their great purpose, the people retain the right to alter their government.

The Declaration says the long-claimed divine right of kings

is a fraud. It asserts that the liberties it recognizes are grounded in a higher law governing all human laws. This higher law derives not only from reason (its truths are "self-evident"), but also from revelation—the Declaration refers to God four times, using such Deistic terms as "Supreme Judge of the world." Today, the extraordinary proliferation of creeds and denominations of religions in America suggests that the Judeo-Christian tradition is alive and thriving in the United States. Indeed, a recent Gallup Poll reported that 85 percent of Americans believe that religion is an important part of their lives.

If the Declaration had simply announced the independence of certain disaffected British colonials, it would be long forgotten. What made it revolutionary was that these rebels appealed to a universal higher standard of justice on which they promised to base their government. This is what Abraham Lincoln meant when he extolled Jefferson as "the man who, in the concrete pressure of a struggle for national independence by a single people, had the coolness, forecast, and capacity to introduce into a merely revolutionary document, an abstract truth, applicable to all men and all times."

Long before he became president, Lincoln focused on what he considered the sacredness of our country's commitment to a higher law. As he put it in a speech in Chicago in 1858: "We live in an age of science and of abounding accumulation of material things. These did not create our Declaration. Our Declaration created them. The things of the spirit come first. Unless we cling to that, all our material prosperity, overwhelming though it may appear, will turn to a barren scepter in our grasp. If we are to maintain the great heritage which has been bequeathed to us, we must be like-minded as the fathers who created it. We must not sink into a pagan materialism. We must cultivate the reverence which they had for the things that are holy. We must follow the spiritual and moral leadership which they showed. We must keep replenished, that they may glow with a more compelling flame, the altar fires before which they worshiped."

In other words, the American Dream is more than a good job, a nice house, a loving spouse, great kids, and a hefty 401(k) account. Those blessings have been purchased with the sacrifices of our ancestors. In return for these opportunities, we have obligations. For one, we have to treat others as we would have them treat us—in our society, the Golden Rule should be the ultimate bottom line. To that end, we must commit ourselves to protect the God-given dignity and freedom of every individual. We must uphold institutions that nourish personal and public virtues, among them such pillars of the decent life as the family, the neighborhood house of worship, the local school and library, the volunteer fire department, and the Boy Scouts and Girl Scouts.

America is only as strong as the citizens from whom her legitimacy derives. We are a great nation because American citizens look first to themselves when faced with hardship. We recognize a bound duty to look after our family, friends, and neighbors, providing them security in times of trouble. We understand the importance of contributing to our own community—by taking part in school board meetings, Little League games, and Fourth of July parades.

If this vision of America is to endure, we must make sure that our government behaves in accordance with American traditions and values. We cannot allow a nation conceived in true liberty under higher law to tolerate limitless government power; it is a self-betrayal that corrupts not just our leaders but ourselves, the voters who elect profligate leaders with a carelessness beyond belief. We must realize that nothing is more intrinsically un-American than a system in which bureaucrats and school administrators, not parents, make decisions about a child's education; one in which government handouts create generational dependencies; or one in which retirement comes not on our own terms, but rather those dictated by politicians thousands of miles away.

For our part as Americans, the great challenge is to participate actively in the ongoing experiment, breathe new life into the Founders' constitutional vision, and, above all, provide Americans with practical solutions based on the power of our ideas—ideas that have molded America and can now put her back on the right track. We are optimistic, but only if citizens will have the courage to act.

It's up to us. This is our republic to cherish and nourish. Let's get to work.

ACKNOWLEDGMENTS

★ ★ ★ ★ ★ ★ ★ ★ ★ ★

We are grateful to Speaker Newt Gingrich and Attorney General Ed Meese, whose wisdom and unerring instinct for the basic principles of conservatism have kept us on track.

We appreciate the time and TLC of our colleagues at The Heritage Foundation and at Townhall.com, especially to those who have read our manuscript and shared their ideas and criticisms with us.

Mike Needham served as our "invisible hand" and saw this entire project through to completion from start to finish. We are particularly grateful to him.

To Donna Carpenter and Mo Coyle, whose editorial assistance permeates every page of our work, and to our counselor, friend, and agent, the irrepressible Helen Rees, who reminds us regularly that we are all Americans with a real stake in our system, we say a special thank you for all you did to keep us moving along. We thank Joel Kurtzman for his encouragement to pursue writing the book and for connecting us to our agent.

Our editor, Jed Donahue, and the rest of the Crown Forum team have been indispensable for their guidance and sound judgment.

Lee Edwards has advised us throughout the process as we have tried to stay true to our conservative principles while "doing something" about the current situation that confronts all of us in the United States.

Any errors remaining, whether of omission or commission, are ours alone and will be corrected at GettingAmericaRight.com as soon as we hear about them.

Ed Feulner
Doug Wilson

INDEX

★ ★ ★ ★ ★ ★ ★ ★ ★ ★

Index

Bovard, James, 134, 135
BRAC (Base Realignment and Closing) system, 119–20
Bratton, William, 112
"Broken Windows Theory," 112–13
budget, U.S., 1, 8, 88, 93–105, 118, 129, 180. *See also* debt, U.S.
bureaucracy:
  abuse of power by, 52
  accountability of, 2
  and educational system, 23
  and enduring vision of America, 216
  inertia in, 18
  and necessity for government action, 33, 52
  and need for return to core principles, 7
  and responsible government, 106
  and self-reliance, 59–60, 64
  and transportation system, 18
  and waste, 106
  and welfare, 33, 59–60
Burger King, 911 call about, 56–59
Bush, George W.:
  and air-traffic-control system, 40–42
  and education, 44–45, 109
  and MCA, 139, 140
  Naval Academy speech of, 5, 169, 190
  and prosperity, 125
  and security, 166, 168, 169, 170, 172, 181, 183, 185, 186, 188, 190
  and self-reliance, 64
  and Social Security, 80, 81
  and spending, 85, 87, 89
  in Texas Air National Guard of, 116–17
  and trade policies, 142
  values of, 85
business. *See* corporations/businesses
Butler, Stuart, 79
Byrd, Robert, 25
Byrd Amendment, 142

California, 17, 18–20, 173, 184, 203
Canada, Geoffrey, 48–50
Canada, 32, 35–44, 146
Carlyle Group, 172
Carter, Jimmy, 22, 176–77
Carver Academy (San Antonio, Texas), 50–51
Casey, William, 178, 179
Central Intelligence Agency (CIA), 178, 179
change, conservative views about, 5
charter schools, 48
Chicago, Illinois, 61–62, 174, 201–2
China:
  and Clinton administration, 187
  economy of, 11, 140, 167, 186, 187
  human rights in, 186
  military buildup in, 11, 187
  as nuclear power, 164, 184, 186
  political freedom in, 140
  political reform in, 167
  ranking of economic freedom in, 138
  research and development in, 144
  and rogue states, 165, 166
  and security, 11, 158, 164, 165, 166–67, 185–88, 190–91
  and Taiwan, 166–67, 185, 187
  taxes in, 146

  as transparent society, 186
  U.S. industry compared with, 127–28
Churchill, Winston, 4, 157
Citizens Against Government Waste, 89, 91
citizens/civilians:
  irresponsibility of, 87, 113–15, 121, 122
  and security, 183, 184, 188–89
  See also citizenship
citizenship:
  devaluation/trivialization of, 198, 200, 208, 211
  dual, 198, 207–8
  and higher-law legacy, 216
  INS as guardians of, 209–10
  and naturalization process, 203–10
  and need for return to core principles, 3, 4
  as privilege, 209, 211
  requirements for, 194–95
  rights and duties of, 210
  and unity, 194–96, 198, 199, 200, 203–10, 211
Clinton, William J. "Bill":
  and air-traffic-control system, 37, 40, 41
  and budget "surpluses," 88
  and China, 187
  and COPS program, 24
  and line-item veto, 120, 121
  and responsible government, 88
  and welfare, 73–74, 75
Coburn, Tom, 92
cold war, 177–81, 188
Collins, Susan, 102
Commerce Appropriations Committee (U.S. Senate), 25
Commerce Department, U.S., 134
Community Oriented Policing Services (COPS), 24–25
competition, 8, 10, 127. *See also* trade
compromise, importance of, 7–8, 12
Congress, U.S.:
  accountability of, 117
  and citizenship, 203, 204, 208
  and education, 22, 44
  and necessity for government action, 15–16, 17–18, 19, 20, 22, 25, 26–27
  powers of, 21, 95, 120
  and prosperity, 129, 132, 148, 150, 153, 154
  and responsible government, 85, 86, 88, 89–92, 93, 94, 95, 96, 103, 106, 117, 119–20
  and security, 170, 171–72, 173–74, 180, 184, 190
  self-control of, 119–20
  and spending, 85, 86, 88, 89–92, 93, 94, 95, 96
  and transportation system, 15–16, 17–18, 19, 20
  Twain's comment about, 8
  and waste, 99, 103, 106
  See also pork-barrel projects; *specific legislation or program*
Congressional Budget Office (CBO), 99
Congressional Pig Book (Citizens Against Government Waste), 89, 120–21
Connecticut, 18, 45

Index

conservatism:
  definition of, 4
  goal of, 4
  values and principles of, 4–5
Constitution, U.S.:
  and beginning/ending of life, 32
  checks and balances in, 27
  and citizenship, 203, 204
  and education, 44, 45
  and Homestead Act, 68
  and necessity for federal action, 9
  and need for return to core principles, 3
  and powers of Congress, 95
  purpose of, 21–22
  and responsible government, 95
  and separation of powers, 21–22, 27, 44, 51
Contract with America (1994), 120
Corporation for Foreign Opinion Analysis (CFOA), 189
corporations/businesses:
  accounting system of, 118–19
  and agriculture, 130–35, 155
  ethics of, 153
  foreign, 143–44
  and illegal immigrants, 205
  and Pledge of Allegiance, 200
  and prosperity, 126–27, 130–35, 143–44, 145, 146, 147–49, 152–53, 154, 155
  regulations for, 126–27
  and responsible government, 93–94, 95, 118–19
  and Sarbanes-Oxley Act, 126
  and self-reliance, 65
  small, 152–53
  and spending, 93–94, 95
  subsidies for, 130–35, 155
  tax system for, 94, 95, 145, 146, 147–49
  and transparency, 143
corruption, 1, 8, 216
Corson, Trevor, 27
"creative destruction," 106–7
credit cards, abuse of, 101
crime, 90, 198, 200
Crusader tank, 172
Culpepper County, Virginia, sports complex in, 96
cult of diversity, 203, 211
cultural relativism, 200, 203, 211
Customs, U.S., 104–5

dams, 102–3
Dayton, Margaret, 45
Dayton Development Corporation, 171
Deardorff, Kenneth, 68–69
death tax, 145–46
debt, U.S.:
  and accounting methods, 97
  and air-traffic-control system, 44
  increase in, 10, 86, 88
  interest on, 98
  out of control, 1
  and prosperity, 145
  and responsible government, 10, 86, 88, 97–98, 122

and security, 168
and Social Security, 44, 77–78, 88, 118
Decker, Jeffrey Louis, 123
Declaration of Independence, 3, 158, 214–15
defense. See Defense Department, U.S.; security
Defense Department, U.S., 86, 100–101, 157–58, 159, 167, 170, 171–72
defense workers, 71
dental programs, public, 65
dependency, 7, 9, 55–65, 82, 217. See also self-reliance; welfare
deranged man story, 104–5
Despres, Gregory, 104–5
Dicks, Norman, 25
Disneyland, 91
District of Columbia, education in, 45–46
Doha Round, 142
Dong Lu Chen, 198
Drug Enforcement Act, 135
dual citizenship, 198, 207–8

"earmarking," 96
earned income tax credit, 103
economic freedom:
  international ranking of, 136–45, 151–52
  proposals for increasing, 144–55
  and prosperity, 125–26, 136–55
  and security, 187
economy:
  of China, 11, 140, 167, 186, 187
  and dangers facing U.S., 1–2
  government as savior of, 154
  and prosperity, 10, 125–26, 136–55
  and security, 11, 187
  and self-reliance, 65
  of Soviet Union, 178–81
  and spending, 98
  See also economic freedom
education:
  bilingual, 203, 211–12
  and enduring vision of America, 216
  as failure, 201
  and foreign students in American universities, 144
  funding for, 10
  of immigrants, 3, 201–4, 210, 211, 212
  and necessity for government action, 32, 44–51, 52
  and need for return to core principles, 3
  and prosperity, 129, 144
  and responsible government, 10, 86, 108–9
  and self-reliance, 60–61, 65, 69–73
  and separation of powers, 22–23
  and spending, 86
  and unity, 201–4, 209, 210, 211–12
  and waste, 108–9
  and Women's Educational Equity Act (1974), 108–9
  See also GI Bill of Rights; student loans; specific program or law
Education and Workforce Committee (U.S. House), 22–23
Education Department, U.S., 22, 23, 102, 109

223

Index

Index

Index

Index

Index

Index

ABOUT THE AUTHORS

★ ★ ★ ★ ★ ★ ★ ★ ★ ★

EDWIN J. FEULNER JR. is the president of The Heritage Foundation, a Washington, D.C.–based research and educational institute dedicated to formulating and promoting conservative public policies based on the principles of free enterprise, limited government, individual freedom, traditional American values, and a strong national defense. A veteran of the Reagan administration, Feulner holds a B.S. from Regis University, an MBA from the Wharton School at the University of Pennsylvania, and a Ph.D. from the University of Edinburgh. He is also a syndicated columnist, a contributor to *Investor's Business Daily,* and the author of five other books. For his contributions to the conservative movement President Reagan awarded him with the Presidential Citizens Medal in 1989.

DOUGLAS A. WILSON is the chairman of Townhall.com, the leading conservative news and community website in the United States, and C.E.O. of Next Solutions, Inc., a management consulting company. He graduated from Southern Methodist University and holds a doctorate in counseling from the University of North Texas and a master's in theology from Dallas Theology Seminary. He has also taught at the Graduate School of Business at the University of Southern California and has served on the advisory board of Empower America with Jack Kemp and Bill Bennett. Wilson is based in Newport Beach, California.

For more information on how you
can help get America right, visit
www.GettingAmericaRight.com.

For more education on the issues discussed in
Getting America Right,
visit www.Heritage.org.

And for all the latest in news,
opinion, and action, visit
www.Townhall.com.